Diane Wakoski

The Archaeology of Movies and Books

Volume I: Medea the Sorceress

DIANE WAKOSKI

MEDEA
THE SORCERESS

BLACK SPARROW PRESS · SANTA ROSA · 1991

ACKNOWLEDGEMENTS

Poems have appeared in the following magazines: *Agni Review, Alpha Beat Soup, Caliban, Michigan Quarterly, Nightsun, Passages North, Poetry Canada Review, The Portland Review, Raccoon, Redstart, Sycamore Review* and *Witness.*

The completion of this volume was partially made possible with the support of the Michigan Council of the Arts.

Excerpts from *Quantum Reality: Beyond the New Physics* by Nick Herbert, copyright © 1985 by Nick Herbert. Used by permission of Doubleday, a division of Bantam Doubleday Dell Publishing Group, Inc.

The author gratefully acknowledges the permission of Mario Puzo to reprint from his book *Inside Las Vegas.*

Black Sparrow Press books are printed on acid-free paper.

LIBRARY OF CONGRESS CATALOGING-IN-PUBLICATION DATA

Wakoski, Diane.
  Medea the Sorceress / Diane Wakoski.
     p.   cm. — (Archaeology of movies and books : v.1)
ISBN 0-87685-810-8 :   ISBN 0-87685-809-4 (pbk.) :
     ISBN 0-87685-811-6 (signed) :
  I. Title.   II. Series.
PS3573.A42M4   1991
811'.54—dc20   90-22954
                                        CIP

To Robert Turney
Archeologist of Light

TABLE OF CONTENTS

The Map 11
The Orange 13
The Pre-Quantum-Theory Universe 16
The Archeology of Movies & Books 20
Rosenkavalier (Knight of the Rose) 28
Finding the Moon (flowers) 32
Coiling Light 35
Control Is About Possession 40
The Eyes of Laura Mars: An Orchid Myth 43
The Lady in the Garden 47
Jealous Slots & the Tree of Life 53
Nuns 60
City of Lights (Las Vegas) 63
The Last Word on Sex 69
Snow on Idun's Apples 76
The Silver Surfer on the Desert 78
California Girl 81
40° 84
Craig's Muse: Wearing the Green 89
Meditation on the King of Staves (Wands) 91
Medea the Sorceress 97
Salad Flowers 101
Crocus 106
The Beauty of Un-used Things 110
The Dianes 113
5 of Staves (Wands) 116

The Coffee Drinker 125
Morning Star 128
When Breakfast Is Brought by the Morning Star 130
Red in the Morning 134
My $15 Lily 137
Men's Eyes 140
Mint Flowers 143
Californians 147
Corn Lyrics 154
Steel Man 158
Neighborhood Light 162
San Diego 169
Waiting for the New Tom Cruise Movie: Summer '88 ...172
Bad Girl 175
Moneylight 179
Robert's Caps 180
Hummingbird Light 186
Junk Jewelry 189
Champagne.....................................192
Failures of the World............................195

MEDEA THE SORCERESS

Nothing exposes the perplexity at the heart of physics more starkly than certain preposterous-sounding claims a few outspoken physicists are making concerning how the world really works. If we take these claims at face value, the stories physicists tell resemble the tales of mystics and madmen. Physicists are quick to reject such unsavory associations and insist that they speak sober fact. We do not make these claims out of ignorance, they say, like ancient mapmakers filling in terra incognitas with plausible geography. Not ignorance, but the emergence of unexpected knowledge forces on us all new visions of the way things really are.

The new physics' vision is still clouded, as evidenced by the multiplicity of its claims, but whatever the outcome, it is sure to be far from ordinary.

Nick Herbert, *Quantum Reality: Beyond the New Physics*

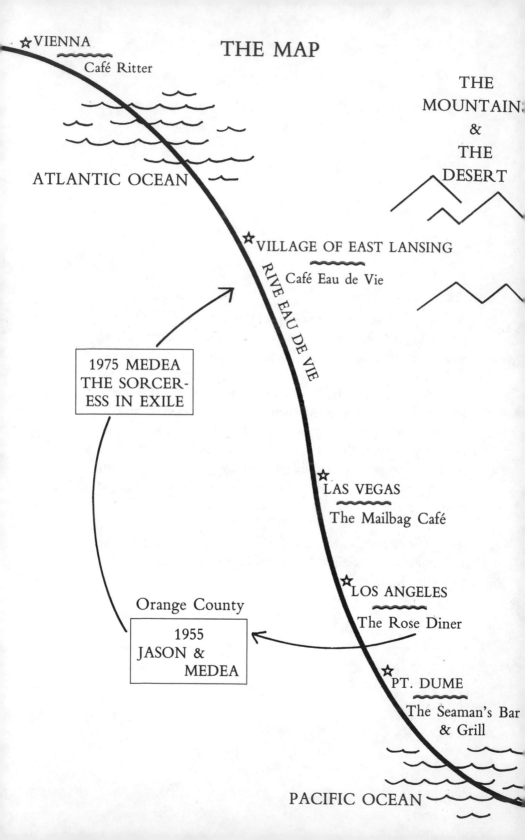

THE MAP

☆ VIENNA
Café Ritter

ATLANTIC OCEAN

THE
MOUNTAIN
&
THE
DESERT

☆ VILLAGE OF EAST LANSING
Café Eau de Vie

RIVE EAU DE VIE

1975 MEDEA
THE SORCER-
ESS IN EXILE

☆ LAS VEGAS
The Mailbag Café

☆ LOS ANGELES
The Rose Diner

Orange County

1955
JASON &
MEDEA

☆ PT. DUME
The Seaman's Bar
& Grill

PACIFIC OCEAN

THE ORANGE

Driving through the desert at night in summer
can be
like peeling an orange,
the windows rolled down, the prickly scent
of mesquite and sage
blowing through the car, the
perfume
of the twilight shadowed earth lingering,
as if the sticky juice
of the orange
were shading and matting your hands,
the acrid spray of the peel;
with its meaty white pillow
nestles into your fingers.

You are driving from Los Angeles to Las Vegas,
running from your loneliness, an empty house,
an ocean which brings neither father nor lover.

For one hour, the wind streams through
your car, a
three-year-old Pontiac you have named Green Greed;
for one hour, the scent of all the desert
plants makes you feel
loved, makes you
forget you have no one

to talk to. You do not care about the
myth of the West, about
the City of Angels and its beaches.

You are not yet even slightly
interested in
gambling.
You are 32
and feel you have a destiny. Somehow
in that car,
on that night, alone on the wind-cooled highway between
        California
and Nevada, for one hour,
the fragrance of sage, especially,
made you complete,
moving swiftly over your face, through
nostrils, the car, you warm,
from desert day fire.

You were not even looking
yet, for Beethoven in Las Vegas,
Snake Mother in the desert.
Your life was over, or
had not yet begun. Did you see
a map of Michigan filling your hand
as you peeled the big navel orange,
the one which glowed like fireflies
that wink
in Michigan summer nights?
The white membrane, the orange raindrop
textured meat of the fruit
saturating your hands with sugar
as you drive, as you drove,
as you remembered one
beginning?

14

Quantum Reality #1: The Copenhagen interpretation, Part I (There is no deep reality.) No one has influenced more our notions of what the quantum world is really about than the Danish physicist Niels Bohr, and it is Bohr who puts forth one of quantum physics' most outrageous claims: that there is no deep reality. Bohr does not deny the evidence of his senses. The world we see around us is real enough, he affirms, but it floats on a world that is not as real. Everyday Phenomena are themselves built not out of phenomena but out of an utterly different kind of being.

Far from being a crank or minority position, "There is no deep reality" represents the prevailing doctrine of establishment physics. Because this quantum reality was developed at Niels Bohr's Copenhagen institute, it is called the "Copenhagen interpretation." Undaunted by occasional challenges by mavericks of realist persuasion, the majority of physicists swear at least nominal allegiance to Bohr's anti-realist creed. What more glaring indication of the depth of the reality crisis than the official rejection of reality itself by the bulk of the physics community.

Nick Herbert, *Quantum Reality: Beyond the New Physics*

For Dante, the first circle of Hell was Limbo, occupied by the good and the great of the past who lived before Christ, or after him but in a place where they had no opportunity for conversion to Christianity. For most of us, life before we discover love, sex and romance is a limbo. And for Diane, it was the world before deep reality. It was

THE PRE-QUANTUM-THEORY UNIVERSE

She isn't the postmistress yet.

She is the little girl in New York City, come there from California on the train for a hot summer in a tenement.

Her daddy's aircraft carrier is stationed in the Port of New York for two months.

It is World War II.

In California she had a victory garden in her infertile adobe-filled front yard, where she grew radishes.

She sees magic in the dark, dusty leaves of the orange trees surrounding her little house.

She makes "oleo" out of a squeeze bag and orange dye.

She plays the piano by ear and wants a kit for making seashell jewelry.

She loves her train ride, wets the bed, reads all the time, books from the library, but doesn't yet wear glasses.

It is 1942.

There are red carnations on her sundress, and she loves her daddy.

*   *   *

There is no deep reality.

Yet.

The Mailbag Cafe,
Las Vegas

Dear Jonathan,

You are neither my son, nor the Silver Surfer, not a lover, husband, brother, or father, but you are big and blond and smart, and more important you love books and those of us who read and write them. And perhaps more important than anything, you understand the power of the letter, not the one slipped under the door and not seen, but the one which crosses deserts, mountains and oceans, dare I say possible galaxies, in order to tell the real stories (the deep reality), to disclose the real histories.

Who am I? I am the Postmistress, so to speak. That is, I own this little hole in the wall here in downtown Las Vegas, called The Mailbag. I named it "The Mailbag" for a number of reasons, the most important being that a distant relative of mine was actually a Pony Express rider, and that gives me some feeling of connection with the history of the post office, of getting mail to its destiny, and of course with being a Westerner.

I don't know quite how this happened, but the cafe has become a place where people who don't want written addresses connected to their lives can have letters or messages sent to them. I am not sure if it is because people who have a cup of coffee with me rather immediately perceive my Romantic nature—the silver shoes I wear with my blue jeans, the fresh roses (in Las Vegas! Yes, this has become a city of roses!) I always have at the tables, the slot machines that will only take real silver dollars, the Beethoven on the Muzak—or if there is some innate poetry that comes to people when they lead secretive lives, but many of my customers receive their mail under what seem almost allegorical names: The Blue Moon Cowboy, Beethoven, The King of Spain, Jennifer Snow, The Silver Surfer, The Woodsman. Or maybe, one by one, they saw or heard the possibility when others came in and asked for their mail. Whatever it is, they must sense that for me the hidden story/reality is the one about how we cannot change our destinies. In my own case, I have never felt that I had any control over my life whatsoever.

When I was a child of about seven, my father's air-
craft carrier was stationed in the Port of New York
for about six weeks, and we travelled by train from
Southern California to New York City to live with
him. This was during WWII, and I remember very
little about that time, except acquiring a little plaster
cast of the Statue of Liberty and carrying it home
with me and everywhere I went for several years
afterward. Lady Liberty. What did that silent icon
have to do with me, my life?

How could I have known then what was in store for
me? What was Oedipus doing when he was about
seven years old? Or Medea? Could someone have told
me about fathers or husbands then? Are they all
betrayers? Or is there only one betrayer possible: one's
own false expectations of reality/Reality/deep reality?
Destiny?
yrs,

Diane, Moon Woman

Einstein and other prominent physicists felt that Bohr
went too far in his call for ruthless renunciation of deep
reality. Surely all Bohr meant to say was that we must all
be good pragmatists and not extend our speculations
beyond the range of our experiments. From the results of

experiments carried out in the twenties, how could Bohr conclude that no further technology would ever reveal a deeper truth? Certainly Bohr never intended actually to *deny* deep reality but merely counseled a cautious skepticism toward speculative hidden realities.

Nick Herbert, *Quantum Reality: Beyond the New Physics*

THE ARCHEOLOGY OF MOVIES & BOOKS

Chinatown is an Oedipal dissertation
on water. The need for it
as a source of wealth. The rich father who sleeps with
his daughter, also
creates, not empires, but
housing developments, by diverting water.
Money is water, no WATER IS MONEY.
This is the voice of desert creatures speaking,
the sparkle of goldwater in their mining eyes. The
daughter of this greedy copulation
is sick and weak, always young.
The detective who searches for the truth
just like the
P
O
E
T, wants *eau, de l'eau,*
and sex,

eau de vie,
but he is lucky/ to get away with his life.

*   *   *

The glitter
and difficulty of friendship
        Dialogism (Bakhtin/Bactine), for the wounds
        to be
cleaned out.
You don't ask me, ever to be myself,
but a bridge between
the Marine Corps march
and all the rest of Montezuma's gold
        Olson,
        Spicer, this time. Fond memories
        of his standing outside
        the poetry readings, telling people he
        didn't like
        to please go away.

POETRY BRIDGES THE PRIVATE AND THE PUBLIC,
no, it is
both. George Stanley, my Pony Express Rider,
where have you been all these years?
Teaching me this,
then leaving,
for Canada;
here I am stranded in the midwest,
my Western boot poised over
another bridge,
this one of ice, The Snow Queen Mother, self
of Moon's hard light. I try
to walk,
but there is no purchase, no grip

21

on this ground, this icy earth,
more water
than steel.

* * *

If Saturn's rings are bits of ice
whirling around his banded globe, then perhaps
it is one of those Saturnian ice splinters
in my own eye that makes me see
The Snow Queen and only The Snow Queen,
his beauty, the
deceiver.

* * *

Cut me an orange,
let its juice soak my mouth and tongue:
I smell the groves of California
and waking to its dusty fragrant mornings.
A ditch where the harmless silver gopher snake
drinks its diamonds of *eau de vie*.

* * *

Distracting melodies, like the sun glinting off a polished
        bumper,
run through my head. There must be
four locations, like points on the compass;
North, South, East, West, can *never* be their designations
though.

* * *

The postmistress was born in LA but lived
in Orange County until she went to New York City/
when she was seven,
wearing an aqua sundress covered
with red carnations. There she got
her Statue of Liberty, a souvenir, then travelled back to the
        West where she
always lived except in a dream.
That dream was Michigan,
a land of Native Americans, Hiawatha's shores
of Gichee Goomee,
but first it was water. All the
water
the desert never had. Still,
it was only a dream, in the shape of a mitten
Water, water, everywhere,
but it was only a dream.
Freedom, Fortune,
they are both ladies,
Lady Luck,
Lady Liberty. No one knows the real
secrets of either.
Or of celibacy, eroticism
that's never (no, always) chosen.

                    * * *

Who is she,
in this desert? Not the Water Commissioner's
daughter, that rich beautiful woman of silk and high
        cheekbones.
No, the daughter of a sailor
who left her high and dry, and her mother,
a bookkeeper for a water company. California Domestic.
Water, water, everywhere. She became

23

The Postmistress,
but never had a photo of herself, like Maximus, standing
in his father's Letter-Carrier bag.
Olson and Baraka,
both sons of father mailmen,
and Bukowski himself,
a postman for 16 years. But she, Diane, of the
hunt
and chase, her quest not venison,
slipping like a silver arrow from Las Vegas to Los Angeles,
water or light,
a sliver of moon,
quick silver, Mercury always whizzing at her
heels, all the days like silver coins,
it is the letters she wants, The Postmistress
wearing her green shade,
at her lunch hour seen in the casinos, waiting
for The Rider from The Pony Express, Steel Man,
or the invisible King of Spain.

* * *

Showers of wheat, at threshing time,
like golden rain: is that what masked
Danae's seduction? Wheat flying through the thresher's air?
Earth/ it is hard to put together
sex and love,
money and life.
When I go to sleep
I am afraid
of never waking up;
cradled in her hand, the little statue of liberty
like Isis or another
goddess of the past.
Imagine Bartholdi in his studio in Paris

with the hollow mold for liberty—
wooden strips with plaster, copper covering it—
a man standing inside a giant hand (not a mitten)
holding a torch as big as an elevator. One
"plaster finger, eight feet long,
lying on its side." What gives each
little bit of flesh its chance
for endurance? The golden crocus peeping out
of thawing ground, bright
against the soaked dead earth.
The skin of an opuntia or little barrel cactus
like a soft animal,
even a water creature like a frog,
suddenly the skin, the soft flesh
holds against itself
a blossom of yellow or white or pink.
How do we get from the stained fingers
and eating barely cooked flesh
to the silk cloth and thread of Chinese embroidery,
gauze scarves, the music of sarabande?
No one whom I know could have invented
the cyclotron, but we all could have tried
to burn gold out of lead. The artist
isn't a physicist
until he has to make
a monument;
change his life from desert
to water.

Dear Craig,

You were once my student and now you've grown
into my friend. Though I call you my Rosenkavalier
and we meet here at the Rose Diner on Melrose
Avenue in LA, our love is the shared love of The
Word, of poetry, not of physical lovers. I see you as
my Knight, and myself as The Lady you serve,
though such medieval images don't actually fit in with
my Southern California heritage and your real life
there in the City of Angels.

When I was young, I fell in love with the story of
Medea. I identified completely with the betrayed
sorceress, with her jealousy of the false (beautiful)
princess whom Jason dumped her for. How prophetic
this tale was to be in living my own life, though at
the time I first felt my passionate identification with
Medea, no man had betrayed me for another woman.
Unless we count my father who left me for his ship,
for the ocean, the Navy, the sea.

Quantum Reality #4: The many-worlds interpretation
(Reality consists of a steadily increasing number of parallel
universes.) Of all claims of the New Physics none is more
outrageous than the contention that myriads of universe
are created upon the occasion of each measurement act. For
any situation in which several different outcomes are possi-
ble (flipping a coin, for instance), some physicists believe

that *all outcomes actually occur.* In order to accommodate
different outcomes without contradiction, entire new
universes spring into being, identical in every detail except
for the single outcome that gave them birth. In the case of
a flipped coin, one universe contains a coin that came up
heads; another, a coin showing tails.

Nick Herbert, *Quantum Reality: Beyond the New Physics*

I love thinking about these poetic theories of the
universe. The idea that many worlds exist
simultaneously explains to me how I can be living my
middle-aged, middle class life in Michigan while
simultaneously meeting you my Rosenkavalier at the
Rose Diner in Los Angeles and my friend Jonathan at
the Ritter Cafe in Vienna, and also be at the Mailbag
Cafe that I, the Postmistress, own in Las Vegas, or
be meeting all of you at the Cafe Eau de Vie in
Michigan. I can still be the young girl, the teenager
who identified with Medea, and simultaneously, the
sorceress who escaped and who is now beyond all
that.
Jonathan told me that he goes to Munich sometimes
to visit a beautiful woman friend who lives there, and
that the train he takes is called The Rosenkavalier. I
was meditating on this for a while this morning,
while waiting for you here at the Rose Diner.

ROSENKAVALIER (KNIGHT OF THE ROSE)

You ride this
train from Vienna to Munich
    — Wien–München —
A woman who wears only a black
lacy garter belt is waiting at the
end of the line/ no,
she has also a dog, a white spade-faced
bull terrier. "Greetings from your father
who passed this way recently," she says
and this reveals she is a fraud.

But she is so beautiful.
"Wait, before you dismiss me,"
she says in German.
It is too painful. You don't
want to wait; you know she isn't
really a fraud. It's just that she comes
from another world, a world of Boothe cartoons,
framed, a world of marble green fountain pens
filled with Pelikan ink, a swirl of
fingerprints like ghost faces
of unborn characters.

Famous for 15 minutes.
Postmodern fate.
Steel Man offers The Silver Surfer

some of his popcorn, but movie theaters
defraud you; they draw you into a world
which is only light play. No matter how many
times you watch a flick, it is never more
than a woman wearing a black lacy
garter belt over her creamy linen-finish
bond paper thighs; never more than
this beautiful woman meeting you at the
train station in Vienna
with her, also white as paper, sweet
dog on a leash, his paws like splayed
garlic bulbs, nails clicking on
the stone floors of the train station;
never more than images which seem
less interesting, each time that you see them.
You leave the theater fat
from the popcorn and thin
from the film which has no angels,
no devils, but is a fraud. "Wait, before you dismiss
it," I hear Maverick calling over
my shoulder.

"Tom Cruise," I reply, "you will never top
Top Gun." Even if I ride this train every day,
you will not come more alive than the first
time I saw you. In fact, Woody Allen is wrong.
Mia Farrow can't bring Jeff Daniels down
off the screen. What she does is
go crazy. She enters the screen, showing
Purple Rose of Cairo, only half there
of course and only half at home.
But sometimes when you ride this train,
you think for a minute
that München and Wien are only
metaphors, not names of towns;

sometimes, you think that the Rosenkavalier
stops in Beverly Hills, then goes on
to Orange County and stops in La Habra;
sometimes you think it winds back up
to Altadena, then heads out to
the desert, making for Las Vegas.
What you think
matters.

What you think
is like a movie.

        "I'm at the flicks,"
makes everyone laugh. "No, not Diane!"
They don't know that I am redesigning
my life; instead of the boy who loved
and betrayed me, when I was 18, there is Maverick
shooting down all the enemies and returning to
Orange County with "that lovin' feeling."
He passes me on to John Cusack, who learns
there is "no sure thing," and writes me into his
life where I can "Say Anything," and like Debra
       Winger,
marry "an officer and a gentleman."

Americans invented the movies; we invented
       adolescence.
Teen-age films are
our genius.

This train takes me to the American Desert:
John Cryer in *Dudes* reinvents
the Western, takes me to meet Clint Eastwood
for dinner. Clint Eastwood has a new role;
he is playing Steel Man, a mythic character based on

the life of Robert Turney in East Lansing,
a man who married a poet, who until she met him
only rode trains from one continent to
another. But there can only be
"strangers
on a train," and perhaps
poetry. In movies and books
we shape our own destinies,
call ourselves
whatever we want to.

And I will call myself, Diane, the Moon, the Lady of
Light, and in one of the many simultaneous worlds
I'll occupy I'll tell the real story of my life, the deep
reality. This archeological dig to show the layers of
ascent and descent and one of the guides will be that
one-eyed poet, Creeley. "O love," he says, "where are
you leading me now?" And the echo of the good
doctor, "no ideas [no reality?] but in things."

You do know Creeley's poem, "Kore," don't you?
And of course Williams' obsession with the
Persephone figure, evolving from his early images and
ideas in *Kora in Hell*? Both poets are obsessed with
the beautiful image of the young girl enthralled by
love. So am I, I guess.

yrs,

Diane, Moonlight

FINDING THE MOON (FLOWERS)

this is my broken/
way
    of saying
           ROSES DO
grow on the desert.
           Don't ask me to tell you why
           that glittering city of
           heat and light
           and games,
           rising up out of the morning
           translates me from the drab postmistress, sorting
           her mail, into the lithe huntress
           stalking the 6 a.m. Strip, eating steak and eggs
           in the middle of the night. Sleeping through
           the crowds
           and the evening's roll of the dice
           to rise before dawn and claim the early day.
           Its chances,
           for my own,
                    But I know that every morning
           there is a promise
           rather than a threat,
           and ageing/ approaching death
           do not claim my attention when I am
           in the West.

This morning
walking south to The Hacienda:
in an arroyo close to
the road,
first the smell, almost
like
lily of the valley,
the freshness of a child's mouth,
the skin of a translucent gekko
the white trumpets of datura, like a hundred
silver moons which have tumbled from a slot
machine,
mounded green
leaves swarming out of a spot
that has held water. I look down
to this oracle of flowers,
my foot like moonlight
carrying me along the road, the desert
in its rose of dawn,
the beginning and end of a ROSE-y tale
I could tell.

Dear Jonathan,

I've come to the Ritter Cafe in your city of Vienna
today, so that we can talk about the West. And all
my other obsessions. Nick Herbert, in his elementary
book I so love on quantum theory, introduces what
he calls theory #8, the Heisenberg theory, like this:

The duplex world of Werner Heisenberg (The world is twofold, consisting of potentials and actualities.) Most physicists believe in the Copenhagen interpretation, which states that there is no deep reality and observation creates reality. What these two realities have in common is the assertion that *only phenomena are real*; the world beneath phenomena is not.

One question which this position immediately brings to mind is this: "If observation creates reality, what does it create this reality out of? Are phenomena created out of sheer nothingness or out of some more substantial stuff?" Since the nature of unmeasured reality is unobservable by definition, many physicists dismiss such questions as meaningless on pragmatic grounds.

Nick Herbert, *Quantum Reality: Beyond the New Physics*

You know, my husband, Steel Man as many of us like to call him, is a photographer. I regard his profession as the manipulation of light, and I often wonder if my poet's sense of light isn't what some physicist might think of as the underlying deep reality. I know that this is absurd, in terms of physics. I know that light *is* substantial. Particles or waves, it doesn't matter. Yet, the very nature of quantum theory is that everything must either be mathematical or metaphorical. Why couldn't light be a metaphor for nothing. The Wallace Stevens *"nothing that is not* there and the nothing that is" (in his poem "The Snowman")?

Memory presents the same problem. Is it reality or only based on reality? One could reverse that and say that what memory is based on is reality (deep reality?) but that memory itself doesn't exist. At any rate, light fascinates me, and the desert seems like the location of greatest light to me right now, as I live in Michigan.

COILING LIGHT

1953, I suppose.
Orange County.
He's knocking on my door
smelling of middle-class after-shave

A rich kid, a lawyer's son,
with orthodonture
and his own swimming pool tan.
Smart, with bad grades, a smartass
in school. We were so

different; but we both had thick glasses,
and read lots of books, played chess,
and it turned out, were obsessed
with sex. Weren't all
teenagers? I don't know. Not one
word about my sex life passed my lips,
nor did I ever hear another girl talk of it,
until I was nearly middle-aged. And
of course now

I only speak about sex
of the distant Orange County past.

Leap. I want to leap off the diving board
into that swimming pool, and I want to
swim beyond my fear of water and my need
for sex. I want to dive into an ocean
of stories that start with a coyote singing
in the La Habra Heights, the land of rich kids,
in the hills above my house. I want to
forget the twin brother I invented and the
father of my country who never spoke up
for me when the prizes of this country were given
out. What I want to do is turn into the Moon
who is mapped with "Mares," or "oceans"
and to be the silvery body of light
in which all men can swim.

I want to be the water and the swimmer. I want to be
the Moon, the girl with the silver ankle
who disappears just as you try to grasp her foot
"Moon, Moon," cried the one-eyed poet, "when you
        leave me,
I am alone." But the Moon never leaves the Lover, the
Poet. She is there, as quiet as light. I want
to be more
than I was meant to be.
Light. Light. Can anyone want as much
as I have wanted? I draw the light,
I collect it, I pull it towards me. It coils around
my head and shoulders
until any man who looks at me
will see its writhing shapes/ be mesmerized/
frozen,
in its diamondback heat.

36

Jonathan, I constantly think of the fact that I grew up in Southern California, the desert, and am living the second half of my life in Michigan, a state whose major resource is water. From the absence of water to the domination of it. But light of course, in both places. Though, such different light.

I have a fantasy often, which is I think is connected to several of my fears — snakes and darkness. The first time I had it, I was on a subway in New York, and I felt sure that there was a snake somehow coiling around the back of my head, which everyone could see. I am sure this is a Medusa image, very primal, perhaps every woman's fear that she has an aura of power around her head which will frighten (men) others away. The fear of it probably comes from some taboo connected with holding this power. It suddenly occurred to me, as I wrote this poem, that the things we need and love, as I long for light, living here in dark-wintered Michigan, are connected with the things we fear. How powerful we could be if we could put them together.

Yr Lady of the Coiling Light,

DW

The Gabrielino and Their Home

COYOTE AND THE WATER

As Told By The Gabrielino

*Although few Gabrielino examples have been
preserved, the oral literature of the California In-
dians is rich, much of it centered on animal-named
characters. Theodora Kroeber,* The Inland Whale;
Jaime de Angulo, Indian Tales; *and E. W.
Gifford and G. H. Block,* California Indian
Nights' Entertainments *are convenient collections.
The stream here immortalized may be identified as
the Los Angeles River.*

A coyote, which, like all the rest of his kin, considered
himself as the most austere animal on the face of the earth,
not even excepting man himself, came one day to the
margin of a small river. Looking over the bank, on seeing
the water run so slow, he addressed it in a cunning man-
ner, "What say you to a race?" "Agreed to," answered
the water very calmly. The coyote ran at full speed along
the bank until he could hardly stand from fatigue and on
looking over the bank saw the water running smoothly
on.

He walked off with his tail between his legs and had
something to reflect upon for many a day afterwards.

Hugo Reid, *Los Angeles Star,* 1851, reprinted in
The Indians of Los Angeles County (Los Angeles, 1926)

Cafe Eau de Vie

Dear Craig,

Edward Weston's images are so much a part of our culture, but when I looked at the Weston show at the San Francisco art museum a few years ago, I was utterly drawn into the quotations from Weston's *Day Books* which the curator had abstracted and punctuated the photos with. Thinking about the art of light, its manipulation, and the camera eye, including that of Steel Man (two of my husbands have been photographers), I came up with what might be thought of as a political or feminist statement. I am not sure that I think it is anything but Reality.

yr Lady of The Coiling Light,

DW

CONTROL IS ABOUT POSSESSION

*When making a portrait, my approach is
quite the same as when I portray a rock.*

Edward Weston, 1931

If anyone
had ever
looked at me
the intimate,
like a woman touching velvet,
way
Weston looked
at rocks,

if anyone
had ever
touched me
with hand
or eye
or thought
the way He looked
at everything

Perhaps I am free though,
because no one
ever
looked at me
that way.

Dear Craig,

I have been reflecting on the fact that you might be
the only person in the world interested in my real
story, though I feel I have been telling it for years.
Have you noticed that we used the word "reflect" to
mean thinking? A word connected to light, just as
we use the phrase "I see" to mean that we unders-
tand. How our dark Dionysian civilization is built on
light and the Apollonian.

And the mirror which reflects what we observe/ what
I constantly think about is the truth of the camera,
that every image is reflected light. Could the deepest
reality be thought? How unoriginal I am, eh? Oh
well.

You are a true Knight, always willing to fight for
whatever pleases the Lady, though I vividly recall the
battles we used to have about poetic truth. Now,

41

you've learned to kneel (and, I presume, pretend you don't hear me). The truth seems to have so many versions.

Yr Lady of Reflection,

DW

Nobody knows how the world will seem one hundred years from now. It will probably appear very different from what we now imagine. Here's what John Wheeler, a physicist actively concerned with the nature of quantum reality, imagines when he looks into the future:

"There will be no such thing as the 'glittering central mechanism of the universe' to be seen behind a glass wall at the end of the trail. Not machinery but magic may be the better description of the treasure that is waiting."

Nick Herbert, *Quantum Reality: Beyond the New Physics*

Must've been something about making a movie that gave
the people involved the feeling that they were rearranging
the universe.

p. 71, *Puss in Boots,* Ed McBain

THE EYES OF LAURA MARS:
AN ORCHID MYTH

for Adrienne Rich

What if by day I am Orpheus,
singing out of the rose bush, making the bees stand still
as they listen with pollen vibrating on their legs,
and by night, I am Eurydice, breathing
orchid breath, purple shadows
I must follow? Dusk is breath, I enter through
one door tracing my own steps outlined in gold. I want to be
both lover and beloved; I want to be the singer,
and the song. But there is no model
for this doubleness.

Orpheus loved Eurydice so much he went after her
where no mortal can go. And she was fleeing the advances of
        another,
when the hissing viper got her. It was only an illusion that
        he could

bring her back. For some of us, the reason is clear. Those of us
who know there is no myth which allows women
to be the charmed singer, none which allows her to go after
        love. She
can be the sorceress who beguiles loves, or Penelope who
        waits,
but she can never be the poet, singer, questing lover.
History will never let her be Orpheus; she is always
the shadow.

There is then, a woman who will not step aside
for history, and she is the one who is Orpheus by day,
even willingly accepting the masculine role—lesbian, teeth
        mother,
career woman, nun or old maid. But by night, she is
her own beloved, the one pulled down to darkness, the
        orchid earth
where she becomes her beautiful woman-self. Orpheus tries
        to bring
her to the light/ his voice takes him anywhere.
But he turns as the first ray of morning, like daffodil
cracks the dark. He turns, and she/
she disappears. She can never appear, for she and he
are one. While he is Orpheus, she does not exist, except in
        his mind.
While Eurydice, he is
only a song.

Thus: the new myth for women
who want to be the Orphic voices of their cultures—
Lesbian, teeth mother, strong woman, nun or old maid.
Hidden women, false men, Annie Oakleys all.

And with my orchid-shadowed eyes, I do not love women.
Nor have I ever been transformed into a man.
Yet by day I masquerade
as Orpheus and transform myself each night as I walk
        through
the door into the flower face of song. Is it because
no man has ever followed me,
as he in the myth followed her, that I
describe a monster? Or have we outlived the old
myths?

If we tear Orpheus apart this time, might he
come back as a woman?

Quantum Reality #7 (Consciousness creates reality.)
Among observer-created realists, a small faction asserts that
only an apparatus endowed with consciousness (even as
you and I) is privileged to create reality. The one observer
that counts is a conscious observer. Denis Postle examines
reality-creating consciousness in *Fabric of the Universe*. I in-
clude this quantum reality not only because it is so out-
landish but because its supporters are so illustrious.
Consciousness-created reality adherents include light/matter
physicist Walter Heitler, already cited in connection with
undivided wholeness, Fritz London, famous for his work
on quantum liquids, Berkeley S-matrix theorist Henry
Pierce Stapp, Nobel laureate Eugene Wigner, and world-
class mathematician John von Neumann.

Nick Herbert, *Quantum Reality: Beyond the New Physics*

Rose Diner
Los Angeles

Dear Craig,

I laughed all the way through your poems yesterday,
and your comments on them, your life. Here I am at
the diner, waiting for you, and thinking about what a
nice Hollywood movie we could make of your life. I
can't see any reason why we can't cast Tom Cruise in
the part of Craig Cotter, even though you are blond
and he is dark (dye is part of Hollywood's magic).
You are both nice Catholic boys and quite athletic.
He might even secretly write poetry, and you'd have
that in common as well.

I have been thinking about men and women and your
rather hilarious comments on what I like to call my
"penis envy." I really don't want to be a man. I keep
saying that, but I want to have the right to initiate
action. I want to be the quester, the lover, to play
the role of Orpheus. It is feeling trapped as an
observer that the photographer, Laura Mars, in the
film, begins to take these devastating photographs of
death, almost as an aggressive assault against the fact
that she can only watch or wait.

There is a nice film which I watched on video recent-
ly, using medieval legend, called *Ladyhawk,* in which
two lovers have been enchanted by a jealous (evil)

priest-magician. By day, she is a hawk, while her knight is human. By night he is a wolf, while she is human. There is always a hope at dawn or dusk that light and dark will overlap somehow, and they will be able to meet and embrace as humans, but of course that never happens until the enchantment is broken. I was not actually thinking of that film when I wrote this poem, but rather of my own life. Creeley's poignant cry in "Kore" to the muse and beloved, "O love,/ where are you/ leading/ me now?" has been my cry as well, but no one cares about a woman who feels that way, whereas a man who does IS the romantic figure.

THE LADY IN THE GARDEN

for Robert Creeley

She holds her hawk
crowned with a hood, on
her hand which is always
shrouded with the leaded glove.

I want
to be sitting
in this Lady's garden,

in a swing with the ruffles
of white cherries frothing against
my elbows and knees. I want to be the one
whose naked foot and gold encircled
ankle makes men Follow her
anywhere. I want to hear my knight, my
husband, my lover, my father, my
brother, saying to me,
"O love, where are you leading me?"
and now I want to run like light
reflecting from an emerald ring, to run
in Emerald Light, and to know
that he would follow me,
would carry me out from the darkest place,
would offer me the apple, take
the blame, that he would push me high
in my swing and feel that just touching my
petals flooded him with light
and gave meaning to every crusade or
battle.

I have been always
the lover, the
follower. I have sobbed,
gasped and choked those words
again and again, "o love, where are
you leading me now?" wondering what man
could ever have been so tormented by love or life,
what knight, what troubadour, what poet
could ever say he'd offered more
and found so little consent?

There are women
who have power, but they are not

even
my sisters.
Who whispers to me now;
what is her name
that I should ever dream of following her?

I think she is Death,
I think she is the woman
in the garden whom I could never
be. Her falcon treads her wrist, wanting
to please, and I stand only
at the door, watching,
as I have always watched,
something apart from me,
my gold footprint pulsing like a lily,
not yet covered with the last shadow
of orchid light.

* * *

Why, I keep asking myself, do I think I could have
lived my life differently without magic, or the magic
of a different destiny. That is what destiny is:
something unalterable. I'm great at stating the ob-
vious, aren't I. And of course that's why fantasy is so
important. The alternatives.

Your Lady Standing Outside The Garden,

Diane

Rose Diner

Dear Craig,

I've been waiting for you to get here this morning,
watching the people on Melrose. There is probably
not a better street in the world for costumes. We are
of course practically in a movie studio set,
geographically. And I've been thinking about how
much I love Las Vegas and gambling (tho I am hardly
what anyone would think of as a gambler—dollar
blackjack, nickel slot machines, quarter craps, dime
roulette chips. And until recently, I only played slot
machines, partly because I didn't feel self confident
enough to play any other game).

As you know I've thought a long time about why
slot machines attract me, and I suppose that it might
just be an attraction for Other-ness. Still, there is
something connected also to the way I love or believe
in love because I am not just being sloppy with
language when I say that I "love" gambling. I do
love it. I think that gambling is a metaphor for
democracy, and in thinking about gambling one can
think about every aspect of American democracy and
find enlightenment. Gambling is the willingness to
risk responsibility, as democracy allows everyone, in
fact demands that everyone, take part in the respon-
sibility for governing the world. And no one vote can

be worth more than any other, as no man's dollar is inherently any luckier or more important than any other.

Of course, the ways in which we love are never very democratic. If there were ever an elitist proposition, it is love. You cannot make anyone equal in love. You either are loved or are not; you cannot win love, nor can you inherit it; you cannot earn it or even buy it. Luck is the same thing. Love and Luck. Now, Liberty—that might be a different proposition. It probably can be won or inherited or earned or even bought. But love and luck—you either have them or you don't.

I was meditating on the fact that I can't bear to see anyone play a slot machine which I have been playing, even though I have left it voluntarily. I am very territorial, and very jealous, and very possessive about what I think belongs to me. Not at all democratic, actually. If I could change one thing about myself, I would change that fierce temperament which makes me so jealous and possessive.

Or maybe I could change it, but think that it is a trait which protects me as much as causing pain. I do sometimes think we relish our flaws.

Yr Lady of the Moon,
Diane

Slot machine invented 1895 by Charles Fry (American mechanic), leased to a gambling saloon in San Francisco

At the Sahara Hotel years ago, with the casino jammed with gamblers of all types, an anonymous threat came to the management that a bomb had been planted. The Casino Manager got on the loudspeaker system and announced, "A bomb threat has been received; please vacate the casino." Nobody moved. Five minutes later the Casino Manager announced again, "Please everybody leave the casino. A bomb threat has been received."

The blackjack players were the first to go, then the crap shooters (it could be that the dice were cold that night), then the baccarat players; finally the roulette players left. But the slot machines kept whirring and flashing. The players kept thrusting in their coins. Out of the thousand players only four would leave their machines. Luckily the bomb threat proved to be a hoax.

Mario Puzo, *Inside Las Vegas*

52

JEALOUS SLOTS & THE TREE OF LIFE

Because she is from California
and she remembers
soft July apricots humming with bees
and the strawberries
as fragrant as baby hair
in late January,
she began by playing what the English call,
"fruit machines."
Four plums: two hundred coins.
Cherries,
always good for a few.
"The cherries," she
often heard other players say,
"keep you going."

But her husband
taught her to love
bars, the flash of black and white,
like nets on the trees which keep the birds away.
Triple bars:
the last accomplishment before
sevens.

"Gamble" equals "gambol."
To play.

And the children in the orchard
        smelling the fragrance of summer
        apricots, the lovely fleshy fruit
        which breaks apart like
        diamonds that have been properly
        cut, falling away with even,
        flat surfaces
are playing, barefooted,
calling each other's names.

Non-gamblers ask her how
she can sit there for hours
slipping coins into
the slot machines. "Don't you
get bored?"

Never.

And *real* gamblers just laugh
at slot machines. They are
filled with the flush of
blackjack, craps and poker
where you *play*.

"At the machines," they
tell her,
"you just wait
to win. You have no control,
use no skill,
at all. You don't really
PLAY."

Plums, cherries, peaches,
oh those sticky apricots,
the orchards of Southern

California, the orange groves
of her childhood, the gambol of
beautiful fruit.

She does not drink
when she gambles. She laughs
at the image of
bars
and cherries, so richly alluding
to the notion of failed
alcoholics and women; or
even the sad past of teenage
cherry cokes.
And she often thinks she
understands why women
are the principal users
of slot machines:
the interaction with machines —
so cool and orderly,
the testing of patience and
endurance, the job's results,
and most of all the lesson
that,
     except in American idealism,

                          the majority
of life does not
reward you for either
endurance or merit.
It is all chance.

        The change girls
who watch the slot machines say over and
over that a machine might not
pay a jackpot for six or seven months of constant play.
Then

might pay off
two or three times
within days, or even hours.

She often wins the most coins
when she wanders and
slips her money
into the machine for only
two or three plays.

But what she really likes to do
is pick one machine
and monogamously play it; she does
this, because she has found
that playing a machine weds her
to it. And she cannot bear
to sit next to a machine she's made love to
and know that someone else
is slipping coins
into the lipped slot,
pulling the smooth-knobbed handle,
waiting for the bars to spread
themselves across
one line in symmetry,
burning brightly in the forest
of the casino night;
when her machine rings
its pay to another,
she cannot bear it.

It is not greed,
unless jealousy is greed.
It is possession, love,
the kind of love that is
possession. She

cannot bear to share it. She goes away
when she stops playing
a machine. She doesn't want to think
of anyone else playing it.

That explains why she will stay at one machine
which is silent, unyielding, ringing not even
a few coins of payback,
once she's chosen it.
Will put roll after roll of
coin
Into It, when It Is
clear,
even to her,
that it will not offer
anything. No jackpot at all.

But in California,
the orchards are never covered with snow.
Even without rings on their fingers,
the children read the orchard
which is summer's book,
sports book, where the peculiar odds require large bets in
        order
to win at all.
This book must be read over and over,
and then remembered,
like the time she waited for a
favorite fruit machine, put in
ten coins as soon as the fat man playing it left,
and hit
three sevens. It paid
her eleven hundred dollars;
and she knew
it was because she'd been faithful,

come back, but
everyone else said,
"You are really lucky."

Because she is from California, she knows
rose bushes, and camellias
whose petals turn brown with a drop of water.
Navels, valencias, cling peaches, black cherries;
her plums are warm, not cool and icy like the Dr.'s.
No apples — the climate's not right.
In this garden, temptation's not
the issue.

Offer her any fruit, the apple even
from the Tree of Knowledge; the one
she still knows no reason

not to eat.

The Mailbag Cafe

Dear Craig,

After you left Las Vegas this week to go back to
work, something strange happened to me. I don't
know if you will think it is strange, but it troubled
me immensely and yet it doesn't seem to mean
anything to anyone but me.

I sat down at a blackjack table and the dealer, who was a chatty fellow, was obviously keeping his job interesting by talking to the players. He was guessing people's occupations, and right after I sat down at the table, he turned to me and said, "I know. You're a nun." Everyone at the table sort of gasped. This seemed taboo, or in bad taste, somehow, and I was stunned. I have to say that I was insulted, though I realize now that part of my lifetime obsession with sex must have something to do with feeling that a woman who does not have a successful sex life is somehow a failed woman. My image of my mother, alone, with my father gone all the time, is an image of emptiness and failure. I have always felt that I had to be with a man in order to be complete, and much as I might admire women who can be alone, some part of me thinks they are failures. I cannot in my deepest sense believe they have chosen to be alone. To choose to be a nun seems almost unthinkable. But of course I am not a Catholic, and you are a good Catholic boy, so you may understand all this better than I.

I continued to be obsessed with the idea that if a man does not desire a woman, there is something wrong with her. And to be publicly identified by this young man as someone whom he could not see as sexual seemed awful. Insulting. Part of the female dread of ageing is that no one sees an old woman as sexually desirable. Even her husband, I think. If they continue to have sex, he sees her, I feel sure, as her younger

self, not her 70-year-old self (or even 50, probably).
So, I suppose that I just looked like an over-50
woman to this young man. Neutral. Neutered? Since
you are my Knight, and I your Lady, I am sure you
probably have some other interpretation of this, to
me, horrifying event. Respect? He saw me with
respect. Awe? He saw me as awesome, holy, pure,
powerful? I am sure that neither you nor Jonathan see
me with sexual eyes, though perhaps you at least see
what sexuality I might have had that other men have
been attracted to, or that my husband sees in me.
Well, I have meditated on this a lot lately.

Yr Lady of the Light,

Diane

NUNS

There is a line, a girdle,
the palmists say, which when it shows in your hand
under the slender figure of Venus, means
that you might be a nun. It is a sign of
chastity,
holding yourself
aloof —
perhaps

60

actually only shows somehow,
the woman who does not bear children.

But there is
something in the face
as well. It is not the light
of religion shining out of the clear
unmade-up eyes, nor is it innocence or ignorance.

What made
the chatty blackjack dealer
look right at me
as I sat down in my California Girl blue jeans,
with straight hair and fresh but ageing face, and say,
"You look like a nun."

The whole table gasped at this young blackman's
audacity.

"Next thing to it," I replied. "A
schoolteacher."

I often wonder if my big protective husband
sees me as something pure he needs to
protect,
or what it was
the blackjack dealer felt radiating out
of me, as I sat down at the table to gamble.

When Steel Man and I are in bed together
is it the excitement of my calla lily body
which has just shed, not her black lacy underwear
from a Helmut Knutson photograph, but her black
coarse-clothed habit, the rough black
of Mothers and Grandmothers?

There are people who dress up when they have sex.
I've never known any of them, nor seen much
excitement in makeup or costumes.
But maybe that's because invisibly I wear a starched coif
and small laced black pumps with thick black stockings.
Maybe the men I have known have all
undressed me with their eyes
and been shocked
at what lay under the jeans and blouses or sweaters.

Secrets. What is the nun's secret
that I seem to share when a man looks at me?
I found that line once
on my palm.
To me, it looked like a marriage ring.
On my unringed, though married, hand.

But I have never seen myself in a mirror
the way a man must see me. I am always
Venus, when I look. Pale
and coming out of Botticelli's
canvas ocean. California Girl, I think,
you came out of the sea.
But perhaps no one
has ever seen that reflection.
It is the secret I share
with real nuns — what their Christ must see
when he looks at his
bride.

CITY OF LIGHTS (LAS VEGAS)

Sitting at the blackjack table, I wear my denim jacket
and blue jeans. Nobody sees the snake coiling
around my neck. Nobody, except one blackjack
dealer
notices I have light
around my head, and he sees it
through his sharp lower class eyes: "You're
a nun," he says. I smile and say, "No,
the next thing to it."

How uncomfortable I am that he has seen me,
Medusa,
sitting at his table,
and senses the danger,
his mirror glasses reflecting my face back
to me. Stoney and uncomfortable,
I bet one chip
at a time. The others at the table believe
in magic, as I do not. I play by the
rules to stay even, or a little less. But the big
winners, they have no light
around their heads. They
bet big, don't look at me, the dealer carries
on, keeping himself awake by guessing
people's professions, asking
about their home towns.

As I leave the table with
exactly the same number of chips
I sat down with,
the snake uncollars itself from my neck,
drops to the floor, moves through the casino
and disappears in neon lighted flashing rows
of dollar slots. Relieved, I go to my room

on the 26th floor, and look out over the desert,
the city of light halo-ing thousands of people,
the desert as dark as ancient Greece. I was
born with California light around my head and fearing
darkness, as well as snakes.

At the blackjack table, no one usually guesses
my secrets, until I met this one young
blackman. There's no way he was called
Perseus, or had a cap of darkness, but
in the future I'll never sit down
at a table with a chatty dealer. He might be
speaking in tongues, for all he knows;
but I understand even the language
of birds, and I know
what I am gambling for:
the secret of death/ the secret of life.

One chip at a time. I'm not willing
to bet any more.

The Mailbag Cafe
Las Vegas

Dear Jonathan,

It has been hard for me to learn the underlying reality
of my life—that I am a loner, even though I seem to
need people so much. Especially men. For reasons that
have never been clear to me, other than historically.
One of the luxuries of getting older, for me, is to
find that once sex is set aside, the real pleasure of
people comes from talk, communicating ideas, and is
more satisfactory on paper than it ever can be in per-
son, for one simple reason: it can be prepared, and
reworked, until it is efficient. Or beautiful.

I suppose as long as we are human, there is some-
thing like sex in our lives which is both complete in
itself and at the same time, a dead end, or mean-
ingless, except through the production of children.
The illusion that I have desperately needed sex in my
life (and I do think it is the grand illusion) has caused
all my troubles. Of course, it has embroidered my life
of books and literature too, but perhaps one could say
that sex is like the laws of physics which seem so ab-
solute and complete to us mortals, but which in fact
might mean little, nothing, or something totally
different in a quantum world. The problem seems to
be that you can never catch a complete glimpse of

that deeper reality as long as you are alive, though occasionally there do seem to be mathematical proofs for its possible existence.

This morning, I am sitting here in The Mailbag Cafe, having my cup of darjeeling tea brewed from the first flush harvest of leaves, a small packet of which came to me through the mail from a friend. I both wish you were here, drinking your coffee with me and am secretly glad that you are in Beethoven's city sitting at the cafe called Ritter (the Knight), reading this letter instead. Who ever has such interesting conversations in person, as we can have through the mailbag?

You know, I was disappointed when I reread Walker Percy's novel, *The Movie Goer,* though the more I think about it, the less I know what I wanted the book to do for me. I know that I have avoided movies most of my life, when what I should have been avoiding was sex. In Percy's novel, the movies are obviously so much more important than the sex, that you wonder why the hero needs to ruin his life for sex (or love), or even to consider it. Yet, the movies are like my own view of sex—that it is an end in itself and meaningless in the world of connections, consequences, or what I think of as "the plot of life." Eating and drinking are like sex. So is gambling, which is probably why I've wound up here in Las Vegas. And movies are too. I think I understand why I have allowed myself to get involved with movies at this state of my life. It is because I watch many of them on video, which is a little like having sex promiscuously, lots of it with different people, so that it becomes fucking, rather than either sex (procreation) or making love. That is one way to take the sting out of it, or to render it totally neutral as emotional experience.

Yet, I am thinking today of Woody Allen's *Purple Rose of Cairo,* which really does what I think Percy's novel should do but does not. Show us that when something like a movie is ALL we have in our lives, then no matter how dumb or meaningless it is, we imbue it with meaning, we breathe life into it, we transform it. We make art.

I wonder how different movies are, from books? What the Mia Farrow character in *Purple Rose* does with her trashy grade B movie is what a serious viewer, a Pauline Kael, would do with a great film, a masterpiece of cinema; and it is what we do in literature classes with masterpieces like *War and Peace* or *Tess of the D'Urbervilles.* What she does, seeing over and over again her silly romantic movie, so that the hero finally comes down off the screen and enters her life, is to point out another kind of reality. Or point it out to us. For herself, she creates it, makes it real by observing it as real.

Quantum Reality #2. The Copenhagen interpretation, Part II (Reality is created by observation.) Although the numerous physicists of the Copenhagen school do not believe in deep reality, they do assert the existence of *phenomenal reality.* What we see is undoubtedly real, they say, but these phenomena are not really there in the absence of an observation. The Copenhagen interpretation properly consists of two distinct parts: 1. There is no reality in the absence of observation; 2. Observation creates reality. "You create your own reality," is the theme of Fred Wolf's *Taking the Quantum Leap.*

Which of the world's myriad processes qualify as observations?

Nick Herbert, *Quantum Reality: Beyond the New Physics*

In an odd way, not only is theoretical physics interpreted in this film, but Allen's movie also lends credibility to a contemporary critical theory about literature: that the reader's response is what creates (reality) value, there being no intrinsic (reality) merit in the work itself.

Isn't this dumb, my sitting here in Las Vegas thinking about how much more interesting it is to think about life than to live it? when the very reason I've come to live here is that it is one of the places where I find myself more alive than anywhere other than in bed. Yes, I still can't give up the idea of sex. I wonder if it was my California childhood which programmed me this way?

Yr avid movie goer,

DW

THE LAST WORD ON SEX

for Scott Glenn

The movies must make you
want to move beyond sex. My whole life
has made me want that, yet how can there be
poetry or art beyond sex or death?

In Hollywood, or Washington, D.C., or The Big Apple,
people kiss you
hello.
They embrace you
good-bye.

They even call you "Darling," or "Honey," or
"Dear," but good Catholic boys
know that love has to be earned,
and maybe all the women in America,
who in these late '80s, have been in love
with Tom Cruise, love him
because they know he isn't
fickle, doesn't womanize, or jump
into bed with any woman
except the right one/ American myth,
or Truth?

In the mountains,
where you can hike or ski,
skydive, or ride your horse,
there is always the
breathless
air, and the snakey
mountains. But to some of us
every touch is sexual,
and we long for the perfect one;
is it forbidden, like Lancelot and Guinevere,
Tristan and Isolde? Or is it the
everyday one, of husband or lover,
never completed, or never seeming
complete?

What would make it complete?

We all answer that
differently, but for you
sitting in the mountains of Idaho,
thinking of your relative, George Gordon, Lord
Byron, perhaps knowing that kisses on stage
or screen, or finally even that family touch, lead

you in a circle or
a chain. Biology. Funny that we nuns
and asexual women are the ones who, longing for love
or sex,
see only poetry and truth,
as if we knew that wanting something so much
must make it
an illusion.

The grail,
this cup I drink my morning coffee from,
yes. It's the one.
Who would think to look for it
on this cluttered old woman's table.
But she is drinking from the cup
she's always thought she longed for. And you,
writing of the Sawtooth Mountains
with a Mont Blanc pen
after you pump iron, punch your heavy bag
and practice aikido,
you know that your pen is not "mightier than the sword,"
but that it is
the sword.

I've always thought
the joke of you sexy men
is that you don't like sex, while we
nerds and nuns think about it
all the time. But at either end
of the spectrum you find
the cup or the sword
and in between
the Garden,
the one which renews itself
every year.

It is dark dark dark,
an early spring,
and Persephone wakes up.
A steaming cup of french roast grailcoffee.
Hades has been up all night,
writing poems with his Mont Blanc pen,
about life,
about death,
the Knights who will rescue Persephone
who has been there, all along,
because she prefers night
to day.

Dear Jonathan,

It's a muggy summer day in Michigan, but I have
come here to the air conditioned Cafe, to write some
letters about poetry readings in the fall and to wait
here in hopes that you might come by for a coffee on
this lazy Saturday.

You are right, America has a big love affair going,
with over-40 women. But only JUST over forty. Not
with over-50-year-olds. And I suspect that Jane Fonda
is going to remain an eternal 40 rather than ageing
into her fifties and sixties. Actually, since I will be 52
this summer, 40 seems young and beautiful to me,
and of course that love affair is with thin, athletic and
rich looking women, like Fonda, who never look 40,

and who don't have that collapsing look, at least in photos, that the rest of us get.

I think the media response to Barbara Bush whom they proclaimed as willing to look her age was almost a kind of nastiness. It has led everyone to say that she looks like Bush's mother, not his wife, and it has led most people to think of her as sexless, or beyond sex, which is actually a nice safe image for a president's wife. Safe for the president, that is, because she will be devoted to his political, not personal interests, AND it implies that he has no sex, either, so that his mind will be on business not naughty things. The fact is that women who look their age, look neutered sexually.

By the way, another aspect of feminism which didn't appeal to me was the idea that it was odious to be seen as a sexual object. I think I spent most of my California youth and adolescence trying to figure out HOW to be perceived as a sexual object.

I don't know if you remember this or not, but when I came to UVA the year you were there, I put a poster on my door to identify myself. It was a poster of me, using one of Tom Victor's photographs, and I think it was one with me standing near a motorcycle. I was wearing a miniskirt and dark glasses and look-ing rather provocative sexually (or I think I was). I remember your asking me, after we had become friends, why I put that poster on the door. There was

a little Victorian sternness in your voice, a father
gently suggesting to his daughter that perhaps her de-
meanor wasn't quite correct. I thought you were
being silly, but appreciated also that you were being
protective, and probably that poster had provoked
some of the (male chauvinist pig, as we used to say)
members of the dept to say deriding things about me.
But it was, for me, both a way of staking out some
territory—I am not an academic, but I am just as
good. And I am sure it was that California girl
grown up into a woman who finally, triumphantly,
was able to at least appear sexually desirable. A short-
lived phenomenon for me, coming late, leaving early.
I am sure that part of my fascination for young men,
or younger men is not just my Oedipal involvement
with my father, who was so much younger than my
mother, but also a way of showing the world that I
still have something which attracts younger men. Of
course, what I have is a secure professional identity,
not sex. But in my own twisted way, it seems to say
to the world, I may not look like much (of a sexual
object) on the surface, but see what a sexy man I go
to bed with every night.

I continue to realize that I have always seen myself
sexually, and to wonder how many men ever have.
Was I always that nun which the blackjack dealer
saw? Surely Medea's jealous rage when Jason suggests
that she amenably accept his marriage to the princess
of the realm is partial rage that her lover could no
longer see her as a sexual object (of desire) but merely

as the mother of his children, and now an inconvenient person to be married to. Of course, she should have realized that he married her in order to get magical help in an earlier situation, and now he was marrying the princess to get political help. But none of us can see ourselves so neutered. Sex is often the only power we want.

What a mistake. No wonder we want a neutered president. Sex is trouble. Only trouble. Ageing is terrible for many reasons, but the one which strikes us most forcibly is the loss of our sexuality. The wise, the gracious, the powerful—they must know how to give it up, like releasing an animal from a leash. The rest of us just make fools of ourselves, I am afraid.

Yr (old) California Girl,

Diane

SNOW ON IDUN'S APPLES*

One curve of a cucumber stem, like a crochet hook,
protrudes from a row of peat pellets in my window
        hothouse.
How fast these seeds are showing
their green. March is the damp, still-stunned-looking
time for midwestern earth, but the romance
of Burpee's colored pages splashing crimson dahlias,
silver corn, the spikes of blue delphinium
among the descriptions of new hybrid peppers and tomatoes
doesn't have that old maid's lure
the pictures did in January,
when you expected the world to be white.

It shouldn't be snowing;
yesterday's ground still was dark brown and wet,
the rye grass showing through the front, otherwise empty,
flowerbed. I was thinking "spring"
though I know I didn't deserve it, having left
the winter behind this year, travelled to sunny places
where almond trees were in bloom in February.

Is this March snow telling me something?
You can't pervert the cycles
without losing?

*Idun, in Norse mythology, is the keeper of the apples of immortality.

My mother crocheted when she was young;
now she has nothing to do.
Anyone who winters here did not go around last week,
as I did, saying, "Well, I guess it's spring, isn't it?"
In fact, most of them just wryly smiled when I said it.
No reply necessary.

Women like me, California Girls,
    who flee from Michigan's dark winters,
    marry younger men, wear
    faded blue jeans and spend
    the cocktail hour watching teenage movies while
        drinking diet coke,
imagine our lives, instead of living them.
We should know what nature has in store for us:
snow on the cucumbers,
a blizzard in May or
frost on the tomatoes in July.
We look in the mirror and see blue, crocus-eyed cheerleaders,
but others see us as we are:
last year's autumn leaves, still hanging on the bare
March branches.

77

THE SILVER SURFER ON THE DESERT

L. D. Clark tells the story of hiking on
the Arizona desert around Tucson and
being followed for almost an hour by a
Great Horned Owl, almost as if he
were a skating partner, following each
pattern of his steps.

Greasewood, blackbrush, sage, and
tarbush, the scrub of Sonoran or Mojave galaxies
scrapes past your Red Wing boots. Walking
this land, or skimming past it
in a blue silver car, you
never know who is travelling with you.

This spring outside my Michigan glass door,
I saw a gray cat looking as downy as Teddy Bear Cholla
and wondered if he had been running
beside me as I drove through Arizona in February,
a wanderer, like the Silver Surfer, searching
from galaxy to galaxy for his love.

There could have been, as well,
an owl, or a hawk, flying
over the car as we drove. There could
have been a Barn Owl with his white sweetheart face

sitting behind us when we picnicked on the desert.
There could have been butterflies, the Desert Green Hairstreak
or Common Sulphur, following the car.

The Silver Surfer, like The King of Spain,
invisible in this morning light
must whisper in the ears of the men I love,
must tell them how I need space and love light as the
      infinite expanse
that space has to offer. He must know that

hummingbirds live on
the desert, and my owl says
nothing but thinks the words, "lux vincit omnia."
The hawks surf their own winds, and the hiker
searches for the Cactus Wren. I exchange my body for
a lighter one and remember with terror
the tumbleweeds hitting the car like boulders
as they blew across to Mexico. But the illusion of
this world must be contained in the body of
every lover, and only with love
denied
can you ever see the whisperer.
The whispered "ahhhhh" as the Silver Surfer skims
the sand, the voice of the snake on the desert coming only
as a light whizzing and shuffling of the sand as he moves—
the voices which tell you about light.

An image. The license plate on your sapphire silver car
says "LUX." You are invisible in the driver's seat,
but for a moment I can see you. I know it is an illusion
for you to appear as a hummingbird, the Black-Chinned,
with his crocus purple neck band, and I,
like the Phainopepla, for a moment
black and crested as Medea.

But a flash of the camera eye has captured
some light. What I have seen cannot be
recorded except as static. And though I stand
here at my Michigan kitchen glass and know it is spring,
          and the grey
striped cat stands
also here, mesmerized by looking through the pane
into my kitchen, we both recognize
the invisible Silver Surfer
standing also behind us.
We both know that the cat ran
on his padded feet
next to the winter car
in the Sonoran desert. That someone
whispered in the ears
of both cat and woman,
and that the light which haloed
our silvery-haired bodies was not
indefinable. That anyone
who followed us
could never be lost
in total darkness.

We teach a new physics.
That there is nothing
which does not reflect
light.

CALIFORNIA GIRL

If I had the ankles of Belma Baskett,
thin-boned, like china
made to be clung to
by a discreet gold chain,
        and barely covered by long black stockings,
I'd wear ice-pick-heeled sandals
and skirts rather than jeans
so that my thoroughbred ankles
would always show;

and if I had better posture and, more important,
a good sense of balance, I suppose I might even with my
        thick ankles,
have chosen expensive British or Italian leather pumps
with medium heels and business-like assurance.

But all my life, I, who could look at shoes
and see their beauty with the same attention and interest
that serious art lovers spend with the Chicago Art Institute's
        Monets
or the Metropolitan's Rembrandts,
have had one unsuccessful pair of shoes after another,
settling finally for a decade of Chinese Communist cloth
        maryjanes
which I now realize nearly destroyed my feet

as I walked for hours without support
on city streets.

Boots. I've liked boots, molded to make my ankles look
as if they have a carved shape, or stout Bass or Frys which
        make
it seem as if I'm modestly not revealing
that I have Ginger Rogers's exquisite instep and arch.
Sneakers and workshoes. I have had them too.
And in those times begun to accept
what I'll never be.

Shall I start over here,
and tell you about the California Girl
who was required to be in gym classes—
        always the last girl chosen on any team,
        always a failure, whether it was team sports, the
                softball she couldn't throw,
        or individual sports, the tennis balls which seemed to
                be worse than bullets.
Easy to despise those dyke-ish girls who were the captains
of the team. But not so easy to handle
the pretty ones, with twenty cashmere sweaters,
        perfectly whited saddle shoes
        curled hair,
the ones who flipped perfectly in gymnastics and on
        trampolines,
who hit the ball and threw it well every game,
who danced in Modern Dance class as if they were training
        for
Broadway, and who,
        of course,
became cheerleaders.

I didn't even go to football games
until my senior year
when I occasionally accompanied my boyfriend, the
        photographer for
the school paper; and I certainly knew that it didn't take
        brains
or anything interesting
to be a cheerleader.
But they were always on the edge of my mind.
Always there:
this is what California is about.
This is what American culture is about.
We invented cheerleaders,
along with the automobile, supermarkets, and
blue jeans. What
was wrong with me?

that I didn't know this or care?

The answer, of course, is that I did;
but I also didn't learn to drive a car until I was thirty-two.
I didn't wear blue jeans, now my common garb,
until I was thirty-five; and I didn't discover how much I
        loved supermarkets
until, also in the thirties, I went to Europe and found myself
        longing
for them.

So, why should I be surprised?
Now, aged fifty.
Having finally converted to the only comfortable, healthy,
and fashionable
shoes I have ever had:
        my Kaepa aerobic shoes, which though I do no
                exercise at all

83

I wear for everything.
Trying on a new pair?
Finding that the model I wore through four pairs had been
    discontinued,
that those first good, comfortable shoes,
healthy ones, California girl ones,
were designed
for cheerleaders?

Cheerleader shoes,
notched at the instep for standing on spirited shoulders,
that's what I wore to enter my fifties!
Oh, origins.
Oh, California American girl,
you cannot escape
your destiny.

40°

Agatha, the long-haired calico
from next door, who can
squeeze through a space the size of
a wedding ring,
walks delicately through the November-
bare

garden.
Each glimpse of her
white paws
against the damp earth
and their graceful engine movements
is a sputter of old images,
a face
I cannot forget, the man
whose tool room
was either perfectly organized
or a jumble.
            When it
became too jumbled
he left me for
another lover.

I will not ever see this almost-winter
garden, the neighbor's cat
swiftly and precisely climbing down
from the now empty summer's arugula bed
without thinking of the fact
that living has not prepared me
to die. I failed at all the
tests—lost ungracefully,
always complained and fussed that
things were never fair.

Agatha's white paws,
fastidious little tools which take her often
where she is not supposed to be,
move rapidly over
the dark earth this morning;
the desert motorcyclist
riding at dawn,
the crouched boxer

dancing under the speed bag,
the man who carves messages
on the large waxy leaves of the
autograph tree —
not *te amo*
but *tempis fugit.*

And I watch from the window
while motion is not the
passage of time,
but reconciliation of failed images/
the cat moving
as I never moved,
I standing still,
as I have always stood,
watching,
out of time, out of step,
but not timeless,
only
out of time.

How lonely old people are. How hard it is to make close
friends. When you are past a certain age the juice to love
your fellow man seems to evaporate. And we all know, no
matter what our age, that younger people find older
relatives burdensome.

And so it seems strange to me that writers and intellec-
tuals single out old women playing slot machines in Vegas
as objects to ridicule and use them as an example of our
decadent society. Surely they, of all people, should know
the meaning of pity. I take pleausre in seeing these old
women intense as little children, waiting for cascading
silver to fall into their laps, oblivious for those few hours

to approaching death, the inability any longer to love truly.

Yet they are reproached for not worrying about Vietnam, the coming atom bomb war, the destruction of the world's ecology, the pollution of the stratosphere.

Mario Puzo, *Inside Las Vegas*

Dear Craig,

Every morning, I wake up and say to Robert who is usually sleeping, "I feel so lucky. To be with you. To have my life. To have such a good job. I feel so lucky." And I do, but mostly I feel lucky each morning to wake up at all. I am very happy with my life. Feel so lucky to have my friendship with you, Craig, and my life with Robert and my poetry and all that. But mostly I feel so lucky to be alive, and not in a war torn country, or in the midst of violence of famine etc. I don't want to die. I don't want to suffer. I want to live always peacefully and harmoniously, with my petty gripes and silly human longings, but I want to live forever.

Boring, boring, Diane. It's time for poetry.

I am not a Dionysian. I simply cannot accept the cycles. I want to believe that, as Whitman says, "death is different and luckier than anyone expects" (my quotation may be not quite verbatim). But I can't yet believe that. Will I ever? Why can't we find comfort in our children? I feel, I know, that you will be the young poet and cavalier who carries on my quest. I love travelling with you, searching for poetry, and while I never feel young when I am with you, because we are so much the mother and the son, what I do feel is that we are ageless in poetry together, and that momentarily gives me the illusion of living forever. We are so different, and yet so much alike. Last spring when we were driving to California I felt that we were looking for your muse, but that we were following mine.

The greenness of Michigan is such a contrast to the brownness, and goldness of the West. Cotter's an Irish name, but I think of Galway Kinnell and dark flamboyant men (Tom Cruise?) when I think of the Irish. The black Irish, I guess I mean. But you are the very image of Light. I presume when you are lucky enough to find the right woman to marry, she will be dark, very dark like obsidian, to contrast with your Light. I dreamed once that my hair was composed of light, sunlight, but it turned into moonlight and then into water and I felt as if I might drown in my own hair. Silly. This is certainly enough talk.

Yrs,

The Lady of Light

CRAIG'S MUSE: WEARING THE GREEN

*for my disciple, Craig Cotter, a Michigan boy
who lives now in California*

Craig, those California hills which sometimes
are as brown and tan as smoothly shaved legs
surround you. Girls with orange bikinis
prepare to meet you and Fumito at the beach, Zuma.

As we drove from South to North this year,
munching dried fruits — desert dates, rains from
Fresno, Turkish apricots, Greek fig, nutty fiber,
dreaming of raw fish, rice and the ocean,
those hills were luscious green.

We both know how flat land can be,
but that flat land of Michigan
wears its green like an inspired
Irishman, always with at least a patch of it
somewhere, even now
when winter snow still covers the lawn across the street.

California's escaped light is worn by a beautiful
young woman, with a hand as soft as a snowy owl,
and green eyes, as all romantic-novel heroines
usually have. She has Michigan Cherry Bounce lips,

ruffled with blossom when she speaks to you.
Taking winter's knife, she cuts a lettuce
from the garden; that must have been California.
Putting on her long fluffy coat filled with down,
she steps out into Icequeen-sledded winter;
that must be Michigan.

Who is this sweet woman, Craig,
who puts figs into our mouths
as we drive, and nestles up to us
in downy cherry blossom lyrics
while I am a passenger in your car?

The man with the camera knows her name.
The Woodsman with his axe knows her name.
The poet with one eye knows who she is too;
all travellers can name
her as well; we must know too

that she wears an emerald dress
under her white winter coat,
and in spite of winter, her legs
are brown, without stubble;

sometimes she rides clear across the country,
like an orange poppy, on the hood of the car.

MEDITATION ON THE KING
OF STAVES (WANDS)

It is the salamander
at your foot which interests me
the most.
                I knew a woman
who stepped on a sliver of
the moon, and tho the light splinter embedded itself in her
she only became light-footed, not lame,
and I knew a woman also
who slapped the sun, that fiery ball, back and forth
over the volleyball net, never even singeing her palms
but I never knew a woman
who could keep a lizard
as a pet,
sitting at her feet in dry splendor,
or love a salamander, in its moist salmon-colored body,
as if it might open its small perfect mouth
and utter secrets.

The dry hiss
of the Pythoness
coming from a steamy crevasse in the earth:
who was speaking? Lightning from the sky?
                Some volcanic core of the earth?
What do men know
which makes them rulers? That little salamander at your foot:

that's the secret. Not the wand,
the staff, the scepter of living wood
you govern with. The dragon
at your feet,
so small, moist or dry, desert or swamp,
the reptilian part of yourself which all men have,
which has been stolen from all women, or perhaps
was never given to them?
Which we can only claim, as
a perversion.

Dare I say it?
The secret of the universe:
     civilization comes in two parts,
     the male and the female. Androgyny a perversion
     of this truth. The two MUST be separate,
     yet cleave,
     both must come together,
     yet always
     separate.

This man flaunts his salamander,
and this woman flaunts her moon.
Until they share the power,
offer it to each other in brief, recurring moments of union,
neither will understand
the secret:
     duality,

     equality,

     its power.

Quantum Reality #6 Neorealism (The world is made of ordinary objects.) *An ordinary object* is an entity which possesses attributes of its own whether observed or not. With certain exceptions (mirages, illusions, hallucinations), the world outside seems populated with objectlike entities. The clarity and ubiquity of ordinary reality has seduced a few physicists—I call them neorealists—into imagining that this familiar kind of reality can be extended into the atomic realm and beyond. However, the unremarkable and common-sense view that ordinary objects are themselves made of objects is actually the blackest heresy of establishment physics.

"Atoms are not things," says Heisenberg, one of the high priests of the orthodox quantum faith, who likened neorealists to believers in a flat earth. "There is no quantum world," warned Bohr, the pope in Copenhagen; "there is only an abstract quantum description."

Neorealists, on the other hand, accuse the orthodox majority of wallowing in empty formalism and obscuring the world's simplicity with needless mystification. Instead they preach return to a pure and more primitive faith. Chief among neorealist rebels was Einstein, whose passion for realism pitted him squarely against the quantum orthodoxy: "The Heisenberg-Bohr tranquilizing philosophy—or religion?—is so delicately contrived that, for the time being, it provides a gentle pillow for the true believer from which he cannot very easily be aroused. So let him be there."

Despite their Neanderthal notions, no one could accuse neorealists of ignorance concerning the principles of quantum theory. Many of them were its founding fathers. Besides Einstein, prominent neorealists include Max Planck, whose discovery of the constant of action sparked the quantum revolution; Erwin Schrodinger, who devised the wave equation every quantum system must obey; and Prince Louis de Broglie, who took quantum theory seriously enough to predict the wave nature of matter.

Nick Herbert, *Quantum Reality: Beyond the New Physics*

Dear Jonathan,

It's Sunday morning, and I have come here to the cool Ritter Cafe in hopes that you'd be out walking Nails, and would stop for a cappuccino and a little movie talk. I have been thinking a lot about doubleness, and how much I long to turn all places into one place, so that when I sit down at my desk I could instantly, or simultaneously be sitting here at the Ritter with you, or at the Rose Diner with Craig, or at the Mailbag Cafe in Las Vegas. I know we can do these things in our imagination, and that we all believe there is a dual physical and psychological world that exists, but you take it one step further into magic. For instance, I have always known that I am Medea, not that I acted out her life but that I was she. This is slightly different from Robert Duncan believing he was the reincarnation of H.D. And I hate the idea of splitting my time between places, or dividing my life up into so many different sections, and then having to live each section as it is scheduled rather than as I feel like doing. This is when quantum theory really becomes my fantasy life, in a way.

Quantum Reality #3 (Reality is an undivided wholeness.) The views of Walter Heitler, author of a standard textbook on the light/matter interaction, exemplify a third unusual claim of quantum physicists: that in spite of its obvious partitions and boundaries, the world in actuality is a seamless and inseparable whole—a conclusion which Fritjof Capra develops in *Tao of Physics* and connects with the teachings of certain oriental mystics. Heitler accepts an observer-created reality but adds that the act of observation also dissolves the boundary between observer and observed: "The observer appears, as a necessary part of the whole structure, and in his full capacity as a conscious being. The separation of the world into an 'objetive outside reality' and 'us,' the self-conscious onlookers, can no longer be maintained. Object and subject have become inseparable from each other."

Physicist David Bohm of London's Birbeck College has especially stressed the necessary wholeness of the quantum world: "One is led to a new notion of unbroken wholeness which denies the classical analyzability of the world into separately and independently existing parts . . . The inseparable quantum interconnectedness of the whole universe is the fundamental reality."

Quantum wholeness is no mere replay of the old saw that everything is connected to everything else, no twentieth-century echo, for instance, of Newton's insight that gravity links each particle to every other. All ordinary connections—gravity, for one—inevitably fall off with distance, thus conferring overwhelming importance of nearby connections while distance connections become irrelevant. Undoubtedly we are all connected in unremarkable ways, but close connections carry the most weight. Quantum wholeness, on the other hand, is a fundamentally new kind of togetherness, undiminished by spatial and temporal separation. No casual hookup, this new quantum thing, but a true mingling of distant beings that reaches across the galaxy as forcefully as it reaches across the garden.

Nick Herbert, *Quantum Reality: Beyond the New Physics*

Ah, that the seamless whole allowed me to simultaneously be at school or at home, that both offices were the same office in some way. Robert, I am sure, would not want that. He likes those separations. They are signs of order which he finds most reassuring. They are signs of division, which I find difficult, or time consuming, or which I feel the need to break down.

96

I want to set up this double world, as I experience it, in *Archeology,* but so far, I have not found a structure for doing it. My model is your double world reality in SLEEPING IN FLAME, which people can conveniently interpret as the physical and the psychological if they wish to ignore magic.

I have to turn the Diane character into Medea, and possibly someone else. Medea is a sorceress, so this should be possible for her. The problem is that Diane is NOT a sorceress.

I see Nails tugging at his leash, bored with us coffee gossipers. Wanting his Sunday walk.

Yrs,

DW, First Lady of the Silver Screen

MEDEA THE SORCERESS

She is in the Home for Unwed Mothers in
Pasadena, the only girl who reads poetry. He
writes to her from his prep school, and she memorizes
the sonnets of Shakespeare as she takes her exercise
on the dusty, scrubby grounds of
The Home.

No enchantment changes her life.
She is told by the Social Worker that she has
FAILED because
      she still loves J
      she doesn't regret doing anything for love,
      she doesn't believe she is bad
      she doesn't regret giving up her child
      she believes her life will go on, the same as it has
          always gone on
      she won't talk about her mistakes.

This is the same as being on the desert,
this life in the linoleum-floored room,
eating with girls who have been raped by their fathers,
and girls who got caught but didn't know with what man
and girls who were only 13
and girls who were nurses sleeping with doctors
and girls who wanted to forget everything and join the
      army,
girls who were all pregnant and ashamed and who knew
      they were
wandering some desert, though most of them, most
of us, didn't know
the names of desert rattlers, or moths like the Dusty
      Silverwing, or
about the tiny burrowing owls, or the lingering scent of
      sagebrush
when the night was pure, pure as we knew we still were.

So, as if she were Medea, when the letters came
talking casually about his dates with other girls, un-pregnant
      girls,
she decided that she would have no choice. She
would kill him, and her children, and like the Sorceress
leave for another world, in her chariot drawn by dragons.

She gave up her baby. No regrets. Only the weak
have regrets.
She went to Berkeley, and she told him
to go away. No regrets. Only the weak have
regrets. She flew in her chariot
with all her dragonlady power to Berkeley,
then New York, then the Midwest, and finally to this Cafe
where she sits telling the tale, not of the tribe,
but of herself, and in spite of what others say, she knows
that the song this Silvery Moon Questing Lady of
        Dragonlight sings,
is the tale for at least half
of the tribe.

Strum, Gunslinger.
Hail, Maximus,
Ascent is descent, Dr Paterson,
O, Love, one-eyed poet, where are you leading me now. No
        one should
be at the Home for Unwed Mothers. That is the real
        Wasteland.
These epistles, not Cantos or songs will be for Craig,
        Knight of
Hummingbird Light,
for Jonathan who understands the myth of the woman
        "Sleeping In
Flame,"
for Steel Man, my husband, who loves me at night in his
        invisible Cap of
Darkness,
and for all women, the other half of the tribe,
for Eve who dared to eat the apple,
I write this letter, and sign myself
Diane,

The Lady of Light.

Good Afternoon, Craig,

It's Sunday afternoon, part of my wonderful 5-day weekend, and I came here to the Cafe this morning, where I met Jonathan and we talked about movies. How I love the luxury of these days with all the time for anything I want to do, no matter how idle or frivolous. Today is *Archeology* day digging around in the past and the present of movies and books and my own mythology. And I chanced the possibility that you might stop by the Diner here on your way home from Zuma, or perhaps on your way out to lunch at the Beau Rivage, since I know it is your day off. I will never forget that wonderful meal you and Cynthia and I had there, which led to my meditation about salad flowers. I think often of Cynthia, though I never write her a letter, as I ought. I can't even remember if I ever sent her the poems I wrote this spring with her at the center of the meditation. Perhaps I should type them onto the computer this week and send her copies. Send me her new address, will you? I hope things are going well for her. She is one of those pure, lovely lights, but so vulnerable, and perhaps so wounded.

SALAD FLOWERS

The Pacific Ocean
like a woman's skirt smoothed over
her lap. The sand, blown clean as the Sphinx,
is outside the window, and the black baby grand
with its white keys and these Malibu Canyon people,
none of whom are in this picture,
hold everything in place.

This is a scene
I am asking you
to close your eyes and
see.
Pretend you are a single lens
reflex, 35mm,
and you are recording
this.

Arugula, cress, radichio, some bibb,
dressed with balsamic vinegar. What is
on top? A bell. A yucca bell.
Its petals as thick as any magnolia lip,
and who would think to eat such flesh?
But its flavor is delicate
as the few grains of sand a child
sprinkled over the woman's naked toes.
Her hair, a strand of her hair loosed from the scarf

blows like the tinkling sand against her cheek,
and it is that delicacy, that almost only a tracing,
which she feels that is the
flavor of
the yucca blossom
we are eating, which has garnished our
salads.

Could the scene be the same? Why not? The
ocean somewhere beyond the walls of this
cafe. No less in Bellflower, a real
town, than behind the oaks shading the fence at
the end of my backyard in Michigan. The
ocean is there, whether it is
California or Michigan,
and on this plate of
Belgian endive, of lobster as white
as the yucca bells and a tomato rose, its hushed
flesh almost hidden on the porcelain,
there are four pansies, two white and two
almost black. Oh, the velvet of the petals
should not be good to eat; oh, the velvet of their
cheeks should be for touching as the child
pats her mother's varnished red-tipped toes,
but these flowers too
end the meal
and I eat them.
I cannot believe they will taste good,
they will taste papery and dull,
but in fact
these pansies lie on my tongue
like melting sugar
of some exotic variety which does not burst
into instant sweetness, but instead slowly
seeps like a drowsy moment

on the beach, with one
strand of your blond hair blowing
against your face, with the
child's round little hand
petting your tanned foot, and
the ocean, fluttering its white,
like a printed cotton skirt over your lap.

You are a woman
sitting on the beach.
This camera has focused
on a flower
which is like the ocean
the one remembered
or seen
which is always there. The
black piano playing
Debussy. Have I imagined this, about
eating flowers? Or is it the
woman or the
ocean or
even
the camera
which are imaginary? No,
I know
I tasted the flowers of yucca,
and I tasted pansies
and the child was there
with her flower hand against my lacquered toes.

Yes, women are flowers. There is no way to escape that image, nor is there any reason to want to escape it. Persephone in a field of flowers begins her descent. Williams says it over and over, "ascent is descent," you have to understand the journey underground, you have to understand being in hell before there can be any possibility of climbing out of the abyss. Reality is the abyss, and deep reality is the journey underground. And the ascent—well, that's the reality we can observe, and it is us, the eyes, the cameras, the light. It is poetry. It is everything which is meaningful to us.

Your Lady in the Garden,

Diane of the Moon

Dear Craig,

I've just ordered a cup of hazelnut coffee from the waiter, here at the Rose Diner. I hope you'll be able to stop by this morning to talk again. I have been thinking, as I was yesterday, of Cynthia, and the fact that she expected so much for her marriage, in such a pure way, and thus has had such a difficult time giving up the image of that successful husband whom she helped through graduate school and into his successful life before he dumped her for another woman. That anger at being replaced by another person which is the basis for jealousy—it must be one of the most powerful human feelings we experience. Medea, Medea, her rage. Oh, Jason, you rat.

There is a freshness about Cynthia that makes me compare her to Persephone. As I always have oddball or perverse interpretations of things, my interpretation of the Hades-Persephone story is that she was seduced by him, found him attractive enough to follow down underground. I don't think this is saying that women who are raped want to be raped. After all, "rape" is only one way we translate the Greek word for what happened to Persephone. Seduction is another possibility, or abduction. It implies something which is against one's will, but do we fall in love willingly? And do we do the foolish things we do for love willingly or because we cannot help it—we are compelled beyond our will? I don't mean to be simpleminded, but love does make people behave in ways they wish they had not felt they had to, doesn't it?

I offer hope though.

CROCUS

*(note: this is the flower, they tell us,
which Persephone was gathering
when she was raped/ taken/ stolen/
seduced/ fell underground.)*

Persephone is a girl I know
who calls herself Cynthia. And in California
which is like Greece with its thick whitewashed walls
and its bougainvillea like Cynthia's magenta lips
nuzzling and dazzling those walls, California
whose piney retsina-like coast always satisfies
my Michigan thirst, this Persephone
is in her cotton-sheeted starchy bed
sitting up, unfolding
as datura does each morning,
yawning in the darkness,
rosy with sleep.

Something has awakened her, for California
has no winter, and thus no spring, but 5 a.m.
darkness is cracking, and splinters of Grecian light
remind her of something she's forgotten.

Persephone's an Eastern girl
who lives now in California. Hades, that tall dark

computer wizard who brought her from the East
and has abandoned her and haunted her Arcadian house—
       she can't
forget him, as if he were a lover, a husband, and not
a kidnapper, who snatched her with spring flowers
       the blue eyes of crocus
       the bard-mouthed voices of daffodils
       the peonies who danced at the enchanted wedding.
But there is hope, Syringa Bride, frothy still
in your white sheets. Yes, the seasons are
in you
even in that static landscape of forever blooming
Birds of Paradise. The corridor, dark with pain, outside
your door—some light/yes, you see some light
there, and a memory of a place. A place where you might
have been
before you began plucking that fatal spring
bouquet.

Persephone, anyone who can listen to Winter's voice,
fall in love with the Prince of Darkness, can also
hear many other voices. You hear one
now. I know you hear it
outside your dark bedroom door.
Don't listen to me;
listen to your running feet each dawn
as you circle darkened stucco houses and shrubs
of nightblooming jasmine and mock orange.
No corridor, no tunnel
back to the light
can be
too long for you to ascend just now.
Spring and All
notwithstanding, you
are a Cynthia, who is not wearing the shoes

of darkness, but instead,
hummingbird shoes,
of light,
of light,
of light.

Well, it just occurred to me that her running shoes,
which of course is what she is wearing, since she is
such a dedicated runner, must be just a progression
from actual cheerleader's shoes, which she probably
wore in high school, as of course I never did. I am
probably the one wearing hummingbird shoes, and she
is wearing the shoes of deep reality.

Yr. Lady of Kaepa Aerobic Shoes,

DW

Dear Craig,

I come here to the Rose Diner to think about the
West, as much as anything. Cynthia is interesting to
me for many reasons, but one is certainly that she is
an aspect of me which never got a chance to exist. I
think of her as golden and lovely, as fairy tales are
filled with Golden Things. But instead of having the

charmed happiness of the fairy tale princess, though it seems as if her life started out that way, she has encountered the same rejections and betrayals that those of us who were Cinderellas have. Though she is an Eastern girl (woman, I guess we are supposed to say, aren't we?), she seems like everything Californian.

When Creeley, or other cavalier-ish poets, thinks of a Lady in a Garden, invoking such medieval images, I always recast these ladies into Southern California high school girls. We did, we California girls, grow up in a land that was an enchanted garden much of the time. Cynthia radiates that pure sense of health which I should, having grown up there. But that is the hidden part of me. Much easier to think I might have grown up a New Yorker, and she the Californian.

I believe that Cynthia is trying to teach herself the freedom of being alone, though everything in her education goes against it. Oddly, I have never been able to teach myself that freedom though everything in my education reaffirms that to need others, especially men, is sheer disaster. I think one of the differences between Cynthia and me is that I was never really married to a Hades, and I never have really been a Persephone. Orpheus, yes, but not Persephone.

She is the pure one, the chaste beauty, but my guilty secret is that I am the nun.

THE BEAUTY OF UN-USED THINGS

There is a woman
with the Flemish hands and lips of Cynthia
in this garden of expensive rose bushes,
but she would never hold
a kestrel, hooded or not, on a gloved
hand, for she loves to climb
mountains and camp by the ocean
and she would not be contained, even by
the man who loved her and betrayed her, the one
she longs for as he amasses a fortune in
Africa and drinks himself
out of control.

Gardens are where she thinks
one might find lovers,
and her lips like raspberries
and her nectarine fingers,
and her Santa Rosa cheeks, they are
made for touching/ to be
touched.

Who is this woman in the garden who is not
Cynthia? though she looks as roselike
and coral-tipped. She holds her falcon loosely
as the Poet's mother "who would be a falconress" did not.
The silken chord, the hood and bell, the reminders

which keep the bird pure, not touching a bloody morsel
until the prey is returned to his mistress.

What is purity but a prison?
Wearing banners of freedom, we choose it?
What kind of beauty does the nun have?
the beauty of un-used things.
Who is the Lady in the garden, and where is she leading us
now?

Your Lady of Coiling Light,

Diane, Moon

Dear Jonathan,

One of the reasons I have not been wanting to be
called a feminist poet is that the label seems to lump
all women writers together, as if we have a common
message. I am not even sure that I have a message,
but if I do, it is full of contradictions and paradoxes
and perhaps even baffling. I kow that I am glad I was
born a woman, and I have never once longed to be a
man though I have an almost classic case of what I
call "penis envy" because I really do believe that if my
culture (or biology) allowed me to be the sexual ag-
gressor that I would have had a much more fulfilled
life, one not so ridden with betrayals and certainly not

so filled with waiting for the wrong men to do the right things. If I could have been the one to choose the men in my life, and if I could have been the one to initiate the love making, I believe that I would have married the first young man I had a crush on and lived happily ever after.

I know this makes me sound a bit out of touch. I don't want to be a man, or actually even to have a penis (I guess I don't think about that much, in truth), but what I want is to have been the one who made the choices.

One of the things which has always made me happy with being a woman, in spite of my penis envy or whatever you want to call it, is my name. I have loved being called "Diane." I have loved all the associations with the Moon, and I have loved the image of Athena, the goddess of the hunt and chase (and chastity), with her silver arrows and what has always seemed to me, the image of a chooser. Not a waiter. Not someone, like Cinderella, who must be chosen by the prince in order to have any beauty in her life at all. Maybe the only reason my life has been as good as it has been, and it has been a good life in spite of all the difficulties, is that I was always a Diane?

Yr Lady of the Silver Foot,

Diane

THE DIANES

Spelled variously, the name
is not uncommon. In fact, like a bluejay
it possesses a flashing beauty
yet can be routinely seen in the summer yard
bending and swaying on sunflower heads
heavy as rusty padlocks
on cemetery gates.

There is music in the name too.
It can either be an iamb or a trochee,
rising or falling, it could be
the notes a bird would utter
again and again:
       Die-Anne
       Die-Anne

Often, a name is the only intimate
connection you carry with you
from your mother's womb. All her
fantasies may
have gone into choosing
your name.
Silver.

Silver arrows, or silver sandals
on the huntress's foot. Diana,

drinking the clear water she shares
with slender-ankled deer. Blue jays
noisily watching. This could be a scene
painted like a miniature vista on a fingernail,
scryed on a gene when your mother thought,

Diane, Dianne, Dian, Dyan, Dyanne, Diane.
She thought she named you
for a popular song: "I'm in heaven
when I see you smile. Smile for me, my Diane."
But as old as you get, you never
believe anyone loves you for your smile.
The name though. They might love you
for that name. The goddess of the moon,
with her silvery hair and quicksilver voice,
the huntress who guards and protects
what only she is allowed to hunt,
the courtier with her jewels, Diane de Poitiers,
the song of a bird, one whose wings
flash blue, then silver, then
blind you with the lapis surprise,
or cobalt depth. Some connection,
some genetic bead, a silver
bracelet your mother slipped on your
arm before birth, echoed in the hospital

on the plastic tag around baby's wrist.

Rose Diner

Good Morning, Craig,

I've come here to drink coffee and to hope that you
might come by so that we could talk about poetry, or
sex, or money, or whatever seems most interesting to-
day. I know you guys all think I am nuts when I
talk about my "penis envy" and I am not sure myself,
often, why I am so positive that had I been given the
prerogatives of choice the way men have them I
would have done any better than I have as a woman.
I suppose that is the way losers think: if only I had
been something else, I would have won?

But you know, it's not really about winning and los-
ing. It's about secrets, the way religious fanatics think
that if you understand God in a particular way you
are privy to a special kind of power. I guess I am a
feminist in believing that male culture has some of
that secret power about it. I guess this is the most
controversial poem I have ever written, and women
don't seem to like it any better than men do. But I
believe this. Oh, do I believe this.

5 OF STAVES (WANDS):
YOUNG MEN FIGHTING OR PLAYING
WITH GREEN POLES

The secret
has always been
what men find
to do
with each other. Those great
majority of moments which, like football
and jock itch, and mining
exclude women.

We have so
little.
The hut
where we go
when we're bleeding, and the moon
is swimming or being washed from out between our
thighs.

          Water polo,
          a big sport,
          at my Southern California high school,
          favored by rich kids who lived in
                The Heights with swimming pools
          boys

who drove new Fords when they were juniors
after their sixteenth birthdays, boys
who closed their eyes when they touched
us in those wet places, all
of us hoping their hands
would not come away bloody. But the
lips
always were,
      whether we sang, "Bah-bah-bah-
            Bah-bah-bra-Ann," or
            "My Little Deuce Coupe,"
whether we drank cherry cokes
or milk, or wrote poetry or watched
movies, we walked in our starched crinolines
and lacy blouses once a month to
segregated rooms, smelling like fish
under our deodorant.

But the boys, they had fun
when they were segregated;
when they were alone together
they touched,
    —with jokes,
      or greetings,
          "Hey, man,"
as we never did;
they talked,
as we still cannot;
they found out how to run the world,
as,
    of course,
we do not.

And water polo, those boys
    hitting that big white ball around

in the green-like-emeralds water
            of the FUHS Olympic-sized pool,
Oh, they even knew our secrets.
That the moon they tapped and spun and slapped
around the water was just like the one
pushed out between our thighs each month
            —if we were good,
            —if we were lucky,
            —if we were smart.
Oh, don't tell me, EVER,
that women have secret lives,
or treasures
that no one except other women
knows about.
            Tell me,
            instead,
that the secret is,
and always has been,
why
men find so much pleasure in each
other's company; why women
when they are segregated and together with
each other, have only the menstrual hut,
the old rusty, monthly blood
to share?
or its taboo opposite:
the little clone of ourselves
forming inside our bodies,
etching its face and shape on the moon,
which will then disappear for nine even lonelier
months.

A child to replace the mother.

                    *   *   *

I continue to be baffled by many things, Craig. Including the fact that people, in general, don't understand what a privilege a safe abortion is. To me, the fact that we do not celebrate the healthiness of that possibility and the joy it can give as well as the misery it can prevent—that alone is enough to make me think we live in a very futile and self-destructive civilization, one which does not appreciate its own skills and achievements, can only imagine that everyone wishes to misuse them. And who is the chooser in all of that. At least if you have a penis, you never participate in those most terrible of choices. If the only power a woman has in a love relationship with a man is through her children, no wonder motherhood is such a dire institution. Though I continue to believe that women/girls survive bad families in a way men/boys do not. But that is another subject.

Your Lady of the Moon,

Diane

Cafe Ritter

Good Morning, Jonathan,

I got here early today. Summer is definitely my time of year, and this year has been, in many ways, the best year of my life. You tell me that you've just read some reviews of your novels and they accuse you of being too involved with objects. Too involved with objects! What century do these critics live in? I, for one, proclaim that worldly things will always allure me. That's part of what it means to be an American. And even more so, I think, to be a Californian.

Well obviously your negative critics aren't familiar at all with American poetry or they would know one of our manifestos. From the good Doctor, William Carlos Williams, Dr. Paterson:

> —*Say, it, no ideas but in things*—
> nothing but the blank faces of the houses
> and cylindrical trees
> bent, forked by preconception and accident—
> split, furrowed, creased, mottled, stained—
> secret—into the body of light!

If Creeley is "O Love, where are you leading me now?" the great song/lament/philosophical question of the cavalier poet, then Williams *is* "no ideas but in things." I say it so often in my classes, that I assume my students memorize it. Both phrases, actually.

I can't believe there are critics out there who don't at least accept that it is a great part of the American aesthetic to understand that phrase, "no ideas but in things." I love the rhetorical gesture from Williams too, "—*say it,* no ideas but in things—." Yes, those critics should have to repeat it, say it, over and over,

"no ideas but in things." There is nothing wrong
with loving the material, physical world, unless one
does it badly or stupidly or, of course, immorally. If
we do not love our bodies, they can never house fine
spirits.

And of course, one of my favorite parts of that
passage from the very first book of *Paterson,* is the
phrase "body of light." Yes, light too is physical, and
has substance. It is body, as we are all bodies, and
must acknowledge that before we can understand the
many properties any body can possess. This stuff feeds
into my fascination with the theories of quantum
physics which constantly lead me to metaphysics of
paradox.

You mention Corvettes which forces me to talk
history. When I was a Southern California teenager, I
wasn't a typical teenager. In many ways. I suppose
part of my adult fascination with American adoles-
cence is that I didn't live one, except in very scattered
ways. I was, all my life, trying to escape my lower
class background. I saw what I had in common with
the rich kids when I was in kindergarten was that I
read books and could be quick in school. When you
are little, the rich kids are ahead in school (unless they
are real morons) because they have grown up with
books and educational toys and parents who are
educated and exposure to more cultural knowledge.
This then led me to realize that I could be better
than the rich kids by knowing more, reading more,

becoming better educated. Thus my lifelong snobbery about highbrow things.

So, I refused to listen to popular music. And I refused during the latter part of my high-school career to go to movies on dates (too common). And I refused to speak or think like my common family and, finally, like other kids who desperately needed acceptance. I tried to be my own version of what was high school chic while at the same time, trying to be the intellectual and the one who scorned teen age stuff. So, I never listened to Elvis Presley, or any of the wonderful '50s rock 'n' roll music. I didn't even know the names of most musical groups. Of course I didn't listen to Country Western music, because my mother liked it, and when I fantasized cars, I fantasized foreign cars, because that was what a snob would fancy. My boyfriend drove a new Ford which his father (a rich lawyer) bought for him, and my mother drove an old Ford—my mother never had a new car in her life, though she started driving in the '20s.

Of course when I went to college at Berkeley and became EVEN MORE of a snob, I learned another kind of snobbery, which was the intellectual snobbery which prefers folk music to popular and sometimes even to classical music. I learned about the purity of the common man and all that jazz of the late fifties, and I learned that Porsches or Mercedes were THE cars, and later when I involved myself with macho men, I learned that Corvettes were made of fiber glass and therefore, awful cars (I developed mechanic's snobbery at that period of my life).

I didn't dream of convertibles, either, as a teenager, because I liked to be very neat and my fine hair drove me crazy, blowing around (I would never wear hair spray — another common thing) and I didn't like the idea of being in a car which messed up my hair. You see what a basket case I was at 16, Jonathan. No wonder I want to recreate my life, and no wonder I love these teenage movies where the sex is sexy and doesn't result in pregnancy, and kids have fun without having to worry about turning into Neanderthals or reverting to some lower class slob. If girls didn't read books, they would be stuck with many children before their teens were over, and drunken husbands or no husbands at all, or even worse, dreary ones who spoke badly if at all and had dirt under their fingernails and were not sexy.

Well, I guess I have come a long way, as they say, Baby, to my comfortable, not so terribly snobbish, good middle-class middle-aged life. But I have had to hold myself away from from so many natural things to achieve this simple world and life that you and Craig were born into. One of the reasons I don't regret my life or any of its failures is that I feel that I have recreated myself in a way that is quite worthy of merit, and it gives me a sense of what is possible in this world. And of course, the limitations. Of what is not possible, either. I do count my blessings, and I do thank poetry for making me realize that even if I didn't have the comforts of material things, I would still have that. So much more than my mother ever had.

Still, like you, I am a 20th century materialist, and I know that beautiful things are the natural outcome of beautiful ideas. I believe, more than anything, that the physical and the spiritual must have a balanced and equal place in our lives, but that they complement each other. If form is an extension of content, as I believe along with Creeley and Olson, then the mind is an extension of the body and there is no reason to hurt or punish or deprive that body, though of course there is every reason to discipline it, to train it, to make it work as well as it can. I wonder if those critics who accuse you of being too interested in objects (beautiful objects) in your books would dare say such a thing about Henry James. I suppose they are the same critics who have accused me of only being interested in my tacky, boring love life. They sound like knee jerk intellectuals who somehow equate an interest in objects with a denial of mind or spirit or idea. They sound a little like the kind of snob I was in high school and college, also. Terrified of anything which might be common. Objects are so common. I guess they haven't heard of Whitman, or don't take him seriously.

Well, I am back to "no ideas but in things" and for me the Corvette is the wrong thing. Now, a Mercedes, a Mercedes. That is something which might

give me the perpetual orgasm you suggest Corvettes
implied in your teenage youth.

Well, I see Nails tugging at his leash. As much as
you must miss Bev and Ryder in Connecticut, you
must also have this lovely feeling of whole days,
while they are gone, with no tasks or other people's
needs to interfere with them. I love that feeling in
the morning, that I don't have to do anything other
than sit at the Cafe and talk or read, or idle.

Your Lady of Body Light, who finds all ideas in
things,

Diane, Morning Star

THE COFFEE DRINKER

for Carol Bergé

When I was as new feeling as salamander skin,
when my young feet were daikon radish flesh,
and my eyes used to bare dusty floors and plastic dishes,
I saw your Lower East Side apartment in New York, five
     flights/no

elevator, up,
not as poverty,
but like an expensive old trunk
filled with glass beads, woven textures from China,
or Belgium, silver trinkets, carved wood,
bits of Kalims. Nothing you had
was new, but everything was
from an exotic place, as if it had been owned by a parrot.
The kitchen had bent, once-costly copper pots,
hand-thrown crockery, wooden implements stained and
      scrubbed
with use. There were a million different woods in all
the furnitures, pictures covering every inch of the old walls,
lovely bits of cloth to walk on, splashes of red in the
umber rooms. In each chamber, there was evidence of
daily living. Half a peach saved and resting on the sink,
a yellow plate with three-fourths of a knish covered with
waxed paper and half a cup of that black cinnamon-y
      Mexican coffee
in a thick cup, sitting there neatly, not as if it had been
left for washing up, but for its actual purpose:
to be drunk later when you felt like
finishing it.
It was that saved,
unfinished
cup of coffee
sitting on my own kitchen sink this morning
which made me think
of the half-eaten peach
and our different lives—how you have always
rescued old things
for one inch of the velvet which still has its nap
or saved a little of the coffee
in case one mouthful of its rich oils
might revive you in an afternoon of rejections

or failures.
The empty sweep of my life,
bare surfaces
and desert maps
where one mouthful,
one drop,
one teaspoon, of water—
could not make a difference,
would be lost or not counted
in the desolate landscape.
Scenes of contrasting beauty plague us all.
Is there anyone who at the end must not say, if only in the
spirit of irony,
"I have wasted my life"?

Rose Diner
Los Angeles

Good Morning, Craig,

How I love morning. The renewal. But it is more
than that. I don't like night, though I have always
liked sleeping. But darkness still frightens me, and
when I am alone I have to sleep with a light on.

There is no explanation for any fear, of course,
because fear is irrational. I would like to love the
night, and feel at home in it. How can the moon fear
darkness? But she does. One of the pleasures of the

mind is to give reasons for things which have none.
The source of myth — to explain things. And science.
Well, here's an explanation for why I fear the night.

Your Lady of The Morning Light,

Diane

MORNING STAR

At dawn
when I need the warmth
of comforters
and to be saved
from the exit of night, which like a lover's good-bye,
or the last flick of a snake's tail
disappearing into the rock wall,
I cannot bear to see,

when truckers are beginning to drive
through city streets
and in Paris or New York,
even LA, some people are already drinking
coffee from paper cups,

planning to beat the day, win the lottery,
have another cup of coffee,

I try to go back to sleep,
ignoring whatever insistent hum it is
that has awakened me,
my body not really stirring,
or perhaps like that snake, reflexively moving
to avoid some danger.
Dawn is danger to me,
Dawn is when
the lover left. He never
comes back, and most nights I sleep
past the morning star,
past the steaming coffee of the delivery van
drivers, and the return of the neighbor's
pure grey cats from their night-garden prowl.
I don't wake until the sun tells me to.
Then walk into the morning summer scent

of petunias. Opening the front door,
the spicy fragrance, as if I opened the lingerie drawer
of a woman who never rises until noon.
She thinks I am the early riser,
but I only want to wake
with light. Never before. Wonder now why I even
think, of all those dark drinkers of dawn coffee,
moving in a world I fear.
I close the front door against the day's coming heat.
Maybe that's all the snake was slipping away from,
the last flash of its tail disappeared
into the cool rocky glen.

My mother always said it was "darkest before the dawn."

WHEN BREAKFAST IS BROUGHT
BY THE MORNING STAR

When breakfast is brought by the morning star,
she is imagining that she is writing in a book with white
        pages,
and that her coffee which comes in a thin cup will taste
like raspberries. She has been a lily all night
on a pond, and her white petals fold into a cone
as she sees the morning star who delivers *The Wall Street
        Journal*
folded on the tray with the china cup and the silver pot.

Water lilies, she thinks, but she
doesn't write it down. And morning glories. The book is
        open on her lap,
her thick satin nightgown is folded around her.
Raspberries with cream would be nice.
Her husband is sleeping and on the pillow
his gardener's face, tanned and earthy, moves slightly with
        his
morning breath. He and she dream different things,
but both wake up against petals, both drink a clear glass of
        water,
both descend the stairs and find the morning star has brought
        their steaming
cups, the fruit, the grain.

Sometimes I miss the obvious. But often,
the water lilies break open in the sunlight, and the pond
poses for Monet. But when I stand still, I notice
all the mistakes I have made. I notice also
that I could live forever, and never live my life
differently. I still long for all the things which seemed so
    elusive
and which I made so many mistakes trying to find. When I
    wake up
in the morning, there is for a moment, the sense that
    everything
is possible. That I can rewrite my life,
that I can be a different woman. But then the morning star
serves breakfast, and one sip,
whether it be a dark fragrant tea, or a rich
oily cup of dark-beaned coffee,
one sip and I know that my life
is the same one I've always lived.
New day.

New day doesn't mean new life;
it means that you continue to work out afresh
each day
the story you were always destined
to tell.

Rose Diner

Dear Craig,

Well, what is the story I am destined to tell? I was thinking about the fact that I used to mix up the names Medea and Medusa, and had to look them up to make sure I was referring to the correct one. When I thought about it, I usually remembered that Medea was the heroine of Jeffers' play, but I would still commit a slip of the tongue occasionally. I used to mix up Perseus and Theseus too until I finally simply gave myself a memory device which was that Perseus was the one depicted in a famous statue on the cover of a paperback edition of Edith Hamilton's *Mythology*. He's carrying Medusa's head.

I noticed that people often stumble and have to think whether to say "Medusa" or "Medea" and it caused me to wonder if that terrifying teeth-mother, witch-like character of a woman with snakes coming out of her head, might not be our image of a woman who would kill her children out of pride or scorned love. My identification with Medea might also be an iden-tification with Medusa, a monster but in human form. I see what Medea did as ensuing from jealousy. I think that jealousy is the most monstrous of all human emotions. But I was interested in hearing an art historian and feminist talk, recently, about Medusa being probably a very early female deity, more primitive than Demeter and thus more awe-inspiring. But the image of the snakes growing out of her head would be an image of power, terrible earth power, power that could not be taken lightly, nor seen without a sense of awe.

I read a fine scholarly book about Emily Dickinson by William Shure, called *The Marriage of Emily Dickinson*, in which he studies the way she put her poems together in "fascicles" in order to understand something about her theology, ideology, her aesthetics and perhaps even a little about her life. His theory is that she experienced something in her life which made her feel that her only REAL life (deep reality?), i.e., her marriage, could be after she died, since it could not happen in this lifetime, and thus she had to believe in a heavenly kingdom, and a kind of bodily identity which could occur in the afterlife. Her poems, many of them, are about this heavenly marriage for which she is destined. I was thinking about that and one of her poems in which she uses the ironic phrase "the scarlet experiment" to refer to death. Imagine, thinking of death as an experiment! Truly, she was a great ironist. But all the reds to be seen in my midwestern summer garden called to mind that phrase, "the scarlet experiment."

If I could really believe in the many worlds theory, I could be enchanted by the idea of death as an experiment, though right now, no physics, no philosophy gives me an easy feeling about death. How I admire

William Stafford's wise poems which imagine, like Whitman, death to be something "luckier" than we might suppose.

RED IN THE MORNING,

(sailors take warning).

> *Split the lark—and you'll find the music*
> *. . .*
> *Scarlet Experiment! . . .*
> *Now, do you doubt that your Bird was true?*
>
> EMILY DICKINSON

When the cardinal
comes to the empty feeder
which the squirrel with the broken leg
has just emptied onto the ground
I know it's time.

When, in the same morning
I see the large raw patch on the squirrel's haunch
near his dragging leg,

134

and he limps as fast as he can away
from my coffee-cup clad figure
down the path covered with creeping thyme just
beginning to bloom,

And, at the end of the path, I see
that weed with the small spade-shaped leaves
which is completely covered with a maroon-red blight,
I stop looking at the blooming and crimson
begonias, the flowers of
the scarlet runner beans,
the tiny-ribbed star shaped red dahlia
and summer's frosting, the lush and grateful
red and white impatiens crowding over
their stone edged beds.

No Rappaccini's daughter, I.
But I come here mornings for escape
from the inner rebellions of my body,
from the hospital red smears and knife warnings.
I come to think of nature
not red in tooth or claw.

With my morning cup,
this sailor's daughter gives up the Pacific
and accepts the Midwest ground instead. She
does not need or want scruff and blood. Even the cardinal's
signal beauty seems ominous
as birds break their necks trying to eat from
empty feeders. And she not the filler;
only the Watcher on deck this morning where scarlet
seems at the least
a warning.
Certainly not,
an experiment.

Do you suppose that my destiny always was to be in the Midwest? My mother is from North Dakota. Do you suppose part of my anger with her is my unwillingness to face my destiny? How I hate the idea that I inherited my destiny from her.

Your Lady of The Scarlet Experiment,

Diane

Ritter Cafe
Vienna

Good Morning, Jonathan,

I have just been outside in our garden, before transporting myself here to meet you. You know the desert landscape is one I love but gradually over the years I have begun to get a set of Michigan eyes. That is, I understand now why some people find the West bare or ugly, though I would never see it that way. It is the longing for green they feel, and

summer here in this part of the Midwest, even in so-
called drought summers, is so lush and green. There
is almost a violence about it, which I think put me
off at first, but now I wander in our tiny space, as
drawn to it as if it might be the Garden of Eden. My
husband, Steel Man, is not only an Architect of
Light, he is also a gardener. He loves ordering things.
I guess I do too. That's why weeding has always
seemed like a strangely interesting chore to me.

I want to tell you about something amusing, or I
hope it will be amusing to you, that happened this
morning.

MY $15 LILY

I know you thought I was wasteful
when I ordered one bulb which cost fifteen
dollars, and because such things are beyond your control,
you smiled indulgently at me like a cat who allows himself
        to be
picked up or petted by someone special, though he would
really rather not
have the attention. And planting bulbs

is always a chore, coming at the time when
the garden is dead and dying, when it is no longer
refreshing just to be out there. You hate it
that the bulbs can't be dug up without sacrificing
their bloom somewhat the next season, and that the ground
where they are, stays unturned, violating
your sense of order and care.
So I had to find a place to plant this bulb
which would not expose it, accidentally, to your shovel
or tiller, and the truth is, that I have forgotten
where I planted it.

It must be in the bed
which you never touch, the one
next to our neighbor's garage,
where the lilies of the valley come first
then the spiderwort, the red peony,
then the few irises which bloom.
I must have put it there.
This bulb which cost fifteen dollars
was to yield a lily so dark it would glint with black,
and this fiery depth was something I had looked at many
        times
in a lily growing down the block from us
which vanished when the owners sold the house.

I walk the garden each morning, in the summer,
with my black cup of steaming coffee in hand, inspecting
        each
new blooming plant, and feeling the luxury of flowers.
This morning I saw a chalice-lipped but not at all jewel-like
        red
lily near the back of the untilled expanse which might be
my extravagant one, though I must say it seemed
just like another lily.

The thyme is springy under my shoes on the path,
the basil bright against the black topsoil of its bed,
and the lilies
having neither toiled nor spun, and we not labored either
for they come back entirely, without us,
are ungilded, as ever. Why did I expect one

to be more royal, more lavish, to gleam with blood
just because I paid too much for it? You smile at me, a
        Hollywood
woman, transplanted to Michigan, as I say, "I think I've
        found it,"
and shake your head.
I have refused to wear makeup all my life,
and yet I seem to want to gild the lily.
Just a California girl, out of touch with the seasons,
expecting more of flowers than I do of myself? Still smiling,
        you
say, "No bulb is worth fifteen dollars."

I wonder if I will ever know which plant grew from
that bulb?

It is the garden which gives me the most peace when
I think about ageing, though I get less and less in-
terested in being anything other than the observer.

Yrs,

Lily-Moon, Diane

139

Rose Diner
Los Angeles

Dear Craig,

I've just seen John Cusack in *Say Anything* for the
second time. While I don't think it is the quintessen-
tial teenage movie that *The Sure Thing* is, I loved it
that the heroine is named Diane and that she is smart,
and I can fantasize that the real Diane, the one I was
meant to be or am in some simultaneous world, is
like the movie Diane who is beautiful also. One
teenage girl describes her as being "a brain trapped in-
side the body of a game show hostess." One of the
things I thought a lot about in seeing this film was
eyes. Cusack has wonderful eyes.

MEN'S EYES

When there is something in the air
which makes you turn around,
which makes you think someone is watching
you, and no one is there,
you think of all the movies you have seen

140

and loved, the men you'd like to have following you,
or waiting for you, as you tap tap along the street,
on your way home.

In my living room was a motorcycle,
and the man in black leathers who once rode it
waiting in the dark. Smoking a Lucky Strike,
reading Williams' poems from memory.
Behind the door of the bedroom
was the secret of his departure, a ticket to
another place, and I only imagined him
sitting there smoking, waiting for me to unlock
the door.

One of the things successful movie stars always have
is a way of using their eyes.
It draws the camera to them.
You, the camera, are always drawn to their eyes. Cusack
has beautiful eyes fringed with lashes
that make you want to be held and cuddled by him,
as if you were an animal and he a loving animal owner.

Cruise's eyes always seem to be looking seriously at the
          world
and slightly making fun of it,
drawing you into the secret of what he sees.
He knows how to use them so that you feel as if
he is including you, the viewer. Patrick
Swayze has hawk eyes, like Scott Glenn and Clint Eastwood.
They seem to be tough, surveillance eyes,
steely, and never sharing anything.
They seem intact,
inviolable and infinitely courageous.
You want to possess such men, because
you know they are unavailable. You, the viewer,

are drawn into them knowing that they will lead you
        interesting
places
even though
you could never really be
a part of the adventure.

The man in the darkened living room,
unlike the King of Spain who is that secret follower,
has eyes like Tom Cruise.
He seems to be saying, "Share my secret.
It is the absurd universe."
But when I unlock the door, he is
not there. The whole apartment is empty.

If I were in the movies, there would
be someone watching me, as I tap down the city street.
But in my life, it could only be
The King of Spain. No man in motorcycle leathers sits
waiting for me, and the steely hawkeyes I look into and
        myself
follow,
belong to my husband,
the man
for whom I barter everything—just
for a touch.

* * *

142

I think that something has happened that I did not
put Andrew McCarthy in that poem. You know I
began thinking a lot about teenage actors thinking
about how McCarthy uses his eyes, or how a good
director is able to use his eyes. I wonder if he has
fallen from my favor since I found out that he might
have a drinking problem. What a puritan I am.

I guess that's why weeding has appealed to me.
Puritans like to weed?

MINT FLOWERS

The crush of lavender

this summer the lushness of everything
even the modest flowers tipping each stalk of mint,
crowds into the morning,
and more like liatris or loosestrife
they hover by the side of the house in Michigan
next to the climbing wild rose.
Who would think of bouquets of mint flowers?
This is also the summer of mosquitoes, nets
of them appearing before your face, gloves of them
covering your hands, and this is the summer
when weeding no longer seems interesting to me.

No, I mean it.
I used to love weeding; it was such a way of ordering
the world. Your lover wouldn't make love to you,
or you never got promoted in your professional life,
or your house was constantly falling apart or your car
breaking down, always always too much to do,
but then you go out in the garden, get
down on your hands and knees
and you fill large bags with weeds and weeds and weeds,
and each bit of ground becomes clean, each planted plant
         breathes
with its new space, each square of dark earth looks darker
         and
lovelier like the summer night itself, as you take away the
         weeds,
and you order and order the world, so that it is beautiful, it
is Cleopatra, or Helen of Troy, it is Elizabeth Taylor or
Kim Basinger, and you walk out each morning
after the weeding, when it is cool and dew is like
Tom Cruise or John Cusack's eyes,
you walk in the garden with your cup of coffee
black as the hair of those beautiful boys, and your newly
         weeded
garden is those beautiful women who never face
death or a sinkful of unwashed dishes,
or jobs they hate or lovers who are impotent or bored
by sex.

But this year, I no longer find weeding
the satisfying act
that I know it can be.
Perhaps the vegetation is so lush
that there are more weeds than planted things,
or is it that as I get older
I am reluctant to cut anything

144

so full of life, so growing and burgeoning.
Am I fat
or tired
or lazy
or is my garden different this year?
These almost bouquets of mint flowers floating tall
outside my window. The millennium is coming,
and *The Washington Post* tells me we have all the technology
and resources we need to clean up our air,
if we'd spend the money to do it.

Did I take the wrong turning, as Jeffers thinks that all the
          human
species did? I mean a different, a personal, wrong turning
so that this summer I can no longer
order my life
clean it up? By weeding? By weeding
make it as perfect as a movie?

* * *

I sign myself

Yr Lady Who No Longer Kneels,

Diane

Rose Diner

Good Morning, Craig,

I am so glad you could meet me here this morning,
because I want to talk to you about my new project.
I am going to write a movie script which will be
about my life, or at least one episode in it, though I
haven't selected the episode yet. I suppose that's partly
what I want to talk to you about. One thing that I
have decided, though, is that much of the film will
take place, maybe all of it, on a car journey.
Americans are their wheels, I guess, and especially
Californians. That makes me, once again, a maverick,
a lost calf, out of it. I, like all the other high school
students, took a driver education course, and I even
got an "A" in it, but I never really learned to drive.
The first time I went out with my mother in our old

Ford to drive, I drove off the road into an orange grove, and I was so humiliated (though my mother was nice about it, and didn't scold; simply got us out without a tow truck—thank goodness) that I decided I didn't want to learn to drive at all. So, I didn't get my license, and I didn't get behind the wheel of a car again until fifteen years later, when in 1969 I decided to learn to drive. I chronicle that part of the story in my poem "Driving Gloves."

I still feel more comfortable with a driver than being a driver, and in particular I love to be driven around by a man. All the men I have been involved with have been good drivers, in some cases so good they could have been professionals. I wonder if this means that I want to be surrounded by California rather than BEING an actual Californian?

CALIFORNIANS

"Worship thy wheels. A hunk is nothing without his wheels."

from the movie, Hunk

147

A grey striped cat came to our glass door yesterday,
staring with yellow lynx-eyes into the confusing
pane of reflections. He was
wintersoft, an animal who lives
in a world of four seasons, and spring
was tempting him with different things than it
tempts me with, the flowers for instance
which he cares so little for.

I am a woman who has escaped winter,
being born in Southern California,
and who often flees it when she can, from Michigan.
And I notice what the lack of winter does
to people, if not animals;
it leaves an old coat intact,
while season creatures shed the old one,
grow a new one. In
California, we tan our hides,
hoping to preserve them forever, and the
only new coat we grow is the frequent purchase
of a new car. Each new coat richer and better
than the old one. Thus reversing the
process of ageing, having started with a castoff junker when
    you're a
teen, and ending up with the Caddy or Rolls or a BMW
when you're too old to drive.

Would my youth have been different
if California boys didn't own cars,
if I had not had that second skin to hide my
naked body in? If I stayed in Michigan through the darkening
of each winter, would I, like the striped cat now
be looking in my own mirror, puzzled at the beauty,
the softness, of my body, and the
quickening of new life inside it?

148

Would that account for the thousands of miles
I travel and must map on my skin each winter in the desert?
Or the freeways of my native state? My golden tan wore off
        long
ago. Even a flashbulb bruises me now.

I don't want to frighten away the striped cat
who's still looking at his reflection.

I know a woman who looks in her firelighted mirror
and sees a bear. He is her lover, or
the only man
she loves. But she is wise
with seasons, and carries power around
her neck—the talon of a hawk,
sometimes the
claw of a bear. And
she hangs crystals in her windows
and communes with trees.

She is my sister,
though we inherited such
different powers. I wonder if
the striped grey cat isn't looking
in my mirror window for another woman?
I wonder if
he found my house
by mistake?

The door to the poet's garden
is invisible, but this cat can slip
under the wall as if he were light itself.
My sister would know
were she to see him, whether this cat
ran silently by the side of my car through

all those desert miles last winter. But
I only see
a soft coated creature,
a cat who's lived through a snowy winter.
His coat would not be so soft
if he had spent it entirely

napping by the fire.

*   *   *

In my middle-age, Craig, I have come back to movies
for a number of reasons, but I think the strongest is
my intense desire to understand the power which my
passionate and troubled adolescence has had over my
life. In some ways I have lived entirely as an adoles-
cent, and while that seems particularly American, I
must see myself leaving that behind, and I must see
the possibility too, through fantasy, of retelling the
story, reshaping it, if not its outcome. I want the
many worlds theory to be my deep reality, just now.
I don't have the *hubris* to reject my destiny, I just
want to believe in other enactments of my life,
simultaneously to soften the inevitable blows of
fortune.

I need to talk with you about the teenage movies
which I think are winners and are particularly impor-
tant to me, though I keep shifting my list of them.
Let me try for a basic list today, but this may be
adjusted.

THE BREAKFAST CLUB

PRETTY IN PINK

RISKY BUSINESS

THE SURE THING

SUMMER SCHOOL

CLASS

SAY ANYTHING

DUDES

VISION QUEST

I think I will stop there, because I will be revising it
every time we meet. Two adult films which are
favorites of mine seem to be developments of what are
the dilemmas presented by good teenage movies. *Bull
Durham* which is really about how to be as good as
you can at everything you do while accepting that
you may never be The Best, learning to live proudly
and undefeated as Second Best. The real lesson of
growing up.

And Woody Allen's *Purple Rose of Cairo* which to me
is about the fact that you NEED fantasy as an adult,
to survive real life, because the things you can

realistically dream of and long for when you are a
teenager, finally are shown to be things you cannot
achieve and that fantasy IS a way of coping with an
impossibly dull or difficult life.

Your Lady of the Silver Screen,

Diane

Ritter Cafe
Vienna

Dear Jonathan,

Up early this morning, and at the Cafe waiting for
you. All the other regulars who come here so early
are usually in more of a hurry than I am, and they
usually read a newspaper with their coffee. I like to
sit and think, as you know, in the mornings. At
most sit with a pencil and paper, still enclosed in the
beautiful silence that night and sleep impose on me,
and still feeling close to something inside me which is
partly beautiful because it is still unarticulated. That
paradox — of wanting something but knowing that it
is destroyed/ i.e. consumed, once you've had it. The
desire to prolong consummation, prolong the pleasures

of expectation and savour the climax of anything. Including the realization of failure which is often, more often, the result, than fulfillment.

I am thinking of a James Wright poem with a long title, "Lying in a Hammock at William Duffy's Farm in Pine Island, Minnesota," which is a short, lovely pastoral lyric that ends with the provocative and slightly ironic line, "I have wasted my life." It's the line I quote in the poem, "The Coffee Drinker."

I love the ambiguity in that poem, but, more, I like its message of doubleness—that the successes of one system of values might be the failures of a different system. I think one of the reasons I love these Hollywood (rites of passage) teenage movies is that everything is still possible in a teenage life. Do you know why I am so obsessed with ageing? Besides just the physical reality, the awfulness of it, and my fear of pain, of disease, illness, dying? It is more than just loss of what you have, though that is terrible enough. It is the loss of *your chance* to have something you long for. When you are young, everything is possible. Or almost everything. I cannot understand young people who feel that the world is hopeless, since the one thing you have when you are young is the possibility of EVERYTHING!

My search for the perfect man, the perfect love, Romance, sexual life, has always been emblematic of my search for something else, you know. In *Pretty in Pink,* a wonderful character played by an actress who

153

must be thirty but who still looks like she's eighteen, the wise older woman in the film, is nostalgically wearing her old high school prom dress and dancing to some golden oldie with the star of the movie (Molly Ringwald) and she says, "Wouldn't it be wonderful if we could start old and get younger every year?" I recall my elders always saying that "youth is wasted on the young," but I guess what I think is that we DO start old and get younger every year, and part of what our actual adolescence is about is learning to ignore death, since it is something which happens bit by bit every day.

Your Lady of Moonlight and Teenage Movies,

DW

CORN LYRICS

In La Habra
with its little library, like
a cottage in Hansel and Gretel, and the
American Legion Hall right next door where
the city park began, we had The Corn Festival
each summer.
             Teenage Diane wore crinoline petticoats
under her swirling gathered cotton skirts,
and white blouses, patent leather shoes, she could have

been the portrait of a lady,
Williams' appleblossomed sweet mistress of Spring.

But summer, summer, the season of fruits —
    the ears of local corn which the city bought
    in truckloads, the orange grove ranchers, their hired
    Mexican migrant-worker hands, the American
           Legionnaires
    with their medals, all of us flirting teenagers,
    our younger brothers and sisters on their bikes, even our
    parents who parked their Fords and Chevys neatly
    along the sidestreets —
summer was, for all of us,
Corn Festival time, and we ate those fat
ears of dark yellow kernels with combine swiftness,
rolling the cobs past our teeth until
they were empty of all but a few
maize shreds.

The ritual of mating, eating, conducted
religiously to the tunes of country western singers,
red-bandanaed square dancers in the evening,
the boy with his Tom Cruise-dark hair and square muscled
shoulders, who pulled you towards him
and looked at you behind dark glasses with Hades' eyes, as if
he could never get enough of your petalled skirts
and crocus face, the saffron of your corn-salted lips
on this South Western American ground
enacting the spring and summer story from every culture;
    she, pulled or thrown underground
    he leading her, or snatching her down
    she following or being caught and carried away,
    he taking her, she wanting
    to be loved, he
    following her, she wanting
    to be kept,

he wanting to keep her,
she wanting to return to the light,
he so dark, she with swirling lacy petticoats,
his eyes that she falls
into, dark earth, deep cenotes,
water of those sexy summers,
at the La Habra Corn Festival,
he, she,   he, she,
Corn Maiden, Persephone,
Eurydice, Chac Mool, Hades,
Bad Boys, good girls,
that's what the earth stories are
all about

Now, like the old witch who has lured
Hansel and Gretel to her sugar house, I
eye Hansel from the pages of my
La Habra Public Library book.

They see an old witch
who wants to eat them, their youth,
but I am only
Hansel and Gretel
grown old, and they are myself
when I was the girl in the swing,
the full-petticoated girl
at the La Habra Corn Festival
kissing the boy with the leather jacket
while we watched the mayor crown
my classmate, the La Habra Corn Festival Queen
in one of those California sunsets
that coil around you,
wrapping you in light.

* * *

Ritter Cafe
Vienna

Good Morning, Jonathan,

As I'm sitting here in this place of Knights and Ladies
this morning, waiting for you, I've noticed a teenage
boy come into the Cafe, sit down by himself and
order a *mélange*. He's got a book, but I can't see its
title. He looks very much like the young actor who's
in *Pretty in Pink* (Andrew McCarthy) who plays a rich
kid who almost, but not quite, dares to be different
and to date the poor girl, played by the girl who of
course finally looks "pretty in pink." This boy looks
ordinary, really a bit weak, but like the actor,
McCarthy, he has interesting eyes. I wonder what
this young man is reading, and why he's in the Ritter
this morning? I always wonder what people are
reading. I'm going to get up and go to the bathroom
and see if I can catch a glimpse of the book's title.
My eyes are too poor to be able to read it from this
distance.

Gertrude Stein. He's reading *The Making of Americans,*
by Gertrude Stein. Imagine that! This is lovely,
Jonathan! Oh, here you are at last. I am already in a
better mood. Who really cares if "I have wasted my
life"? In some ironic and literal sense life is always
wasted (used up) by the act of living it.

157

It occurred to me today that the Metro-Goldwyn lion has so dominated American consciousness that we could think of the lion as our national animal. I don't know why I am thinking about that right now. I suppose it has something to do with the predominance of cat images in popular American culture these days, and the cat-like eyes of the boy reading Gertrude Stein over there. My husband and I are both Leo sun signs, in case that might mean anything to anybody.

Yrs.

DW

STEEL MAN

for my husband, Robert

Leather jackets —
you dream of them,
but I dream of you and all the beautiful young
men who wear them, sitting in
classrooms, flashing
on movie screens,

looking at me from posters.
Like lions in the zoo,
always seeming caged, wary,
always seeming to look for a way out
ignoring me and other women.

In your closet there are
already
several leather jackets,
scuffed bargains,
none ever costing big bucks
or cut by trendy designers.

Those air force, bomber jackets,
with the fur collars
remind me of lions, the ruff
of kingly protection
framing men's faces.

I never wanted to be
the garage mechanic, only
to marry him,
never wanted to ride motorcycles
only to love the man
who raced them.
I haven't worn leather
for years, though I used to
in hopes that, as with Samson, the lion skin
might hold for me secretes, secrets no one could
ever guess. But I have only learned
that women's secrets can never be
as precious as the ones men hold to themselves,
the secrets which bind them together in military
leather, which hold them at football games
and make them afraid of women.

Shouldn't those be our secrets?
Samson, Jacob, even George Washington:
they all won. But what lover
ever opened his closet
and found the perfect coat
when what he longed for, what she longed for,
was the lover him or her self to be there,
saying, "Come in, my skin is yours."

At night I sleep with my hero,
the dreamer, Steel Man,
and while I dream that I might never die,
held fast in his big pumping-iron arms,
he dreams of the leather jacket he'll buy
when he wins the Lotto, a lion's skin
perhaps, one whose leather is smooth and tough
and doesn't feel either soft
or human.

Cafe Ritter

Dear Jonathan,

I don't care what anyone says. Even though I don't
really believe that men want something very different
from what women want, I believe they might as
well, because what they want is wholeness and
balance, and what will balance for a woman is the op-
posite of what will balance for a man. Perhaps some

of the lack of understanding we have comes from that. Perhaps violence as well. I keep pointing out beautiful costly leather jackets to Robert, which are as soft as butter. He despises them. In an odd way, he wants his "skin" not to feel like skin. That seems very masculine to me, whereas my desire is to look at hard things (i.e. masculine ones) but be touched by their softness. I am not sure any of this makes sense. And even though I am the "communicator" in our family it is Robert who knows all the neighbors. We really are interesting opposites, such cartoons almost of maleness and femaleness.

You know, neighborhoods, I guess what I think of as suburban neighborhoods, seem like an American essential. It's not that the idea of a neighborhood is American, particularly, but that we always do think of ourselves as big frogs in little ponds. It is part of our democratic vision. It makes us nosy and anonymous as the same time. A few weeks ago I found out that the fat lady down the street was having marital problems because she came to my door with a black eye, wanting to use my phone. I found myself both sympathetic and at the same time feeling desperately grateful that my own days of an abusing husband are over. I also felt strangely critical of her, and realized that for anyone tainted with darkness we have only fear and superstition that it will rub off on to ourselves. I felt the most I could do was let her use my phone. Anything more would invite her friendship, and I knew that I did not want to share even a

crumb of friendship with her. How we cripples hate
other cripples. Philanthropy has to come from
wholeness, wealth, lack of need, I guess.

Yr Lady Who Is Afraid of the Dark,

DW

NEIGHBORHOOD LIGHT

The fat woman whose
husband beats her, and who
lives down the block from us,
lives in darkness
much of the time.
Now our Board
of Water and Light
is installing
new lamps in front of our
houses, and she stands there
in the yard, where her purple crocuses
are covered with a thin film
of snow, and watches the
hard-hatted men
get ready to bring light
to our small neighborhood.

But she, like Persephone at this time of year,
isn't quite out of the darkness yet, no
April light in her tightly shuttered house,
whose small wooden squareness must squeeze her huge hips
and leave them more bruised than her husband does.

I see her standing there on the handkerchief lawn, looking
puzzled at the lights, the globes, the workmen.
She isn't Persephone: light and dark are the same
to her. She is the mother of two very young children
who visibly have different fathers. No mother ever
pulled her back from the dark underground
of her fat-lady life, and no lover, like Orpheus, ever thought
    to rush
down after her and kiss her
out of viper-sleep.

The myth of women
with their healing powers
and their gifts for
regeneration: she has been
sheathed against it.
She's not a woman locked
down in her dark little house;
she is/
            what is she?
    She has hidden her sex in fat.
    She lives puzzled by light.
    She has children to serve her.
    She chooses a bad husband, one who could
    not find a woman.
    She is a disguise. Don't pity
    her/ pity her
    children,
    and pity the child in her

who also never knew a woman/
a woman
for a mother,
pity the long line
of such impure products.

I turn away.
I turn away.
One rescues because of
overwhelming love.
I do not have it.
I would not go down underground for her,
having already stumbled blindly, and
raggedly, through my own winter, to only
just now see the April light
flooding through my house.
Never
would I have the strength
to go down
in darkness again. Never
have the strength
twice
to bring myself
back out of the dark.

Ritter Cafe
Vienna

Dear Jonathan,

The boy who was reading Gertrude Stein the other
day is here again, still with his fat volume of *The
Making of Americans.* I mentioned that he looks like a
young Hollywood actor named Andrew McCarthy,
and I suppose I was thinking of him because he's in a
film—very minor role—about Gertrude Stein and Alice
B. Toklas which was made in 1986 and came instant-
ly out on video, *Waiting for the Moon.* When I visited
David and Annette Smith at Point Dume that year,
Annette gave a dinner party at which there were lots
of film people because they had visiting at Cal Tech, a
filmmaker named Jill Godmilow. I liked her at once,
for her New York-ness, and her directness and her
literariness, which seemed like something I would not
expect from a film person. I found that she has
directed one commercial film about a woman sym-
phony orchestra conductor, and it turned out that she
was working on a new project which was to be a
film about Gertrude and Alice. She talked of the usual
movie troubles. Raising money for the film and all,
but she talked very optimistically that night, and ob-
viously she found her backing, because that is her
movie—*Waiting for the Moon.*

The film is a lovely film, but oddly disappointing. I sometimes think that "serious film" just cannot be. What troubled me finally about *Waiting for the Moon*, is that it is so nostalgic, even the title and the scene which the title is taken from are pure nostalgic drivel, whereas the plot of the film does not require such nostalgia. Of course, this is a film very much dependent on a writer's point of view about Stein and Toklas, and while the script writer (who plays the role of Ernest Hemingway in the film) has ideas about them which may not be historically wrong, they are wrong emotionally. He makes the women and their relationship seem absurd. Basically, I think it is because the part Toklas plays is written as melodrama. Both the actresses who played Stein and Toklas are very good. In fact, Linda Hunt who plays Toklas is brilliant in most roles. I remember that the filmmaker was lamenting that she could not get Pat Carroll, the woman who did the one-woman Stein show for so long and who was so good, to play Stein because she had decided to go on a diet and lose weight and didn't want to look big, heavy, the way Stein was, any more. I do think the Toklas character was shaped by the male writer of the script and the actress simply honored his script. But it seems like such a man's view of Alice B. rather than what should be a quintessentially female visionary. Thus, the nostalgia, or the melodrama, rather than what I would see as a purer kind of feeling.

McCarthy hardly uses his great eyes in this movie at all, and that's too bad, for they are his asset in his teenage roles, where he always appears as a slightly "deeper" character than his buddies. Perhaps because he doesn't act instantly with speech, and during his silence, his eyes move away from the camera as if in embarrassment (for his peers' behavior usually), or with an odd fleeting moment of amusement, and then back to the camera so that the viewer is almost pierced by their intensity which is slightly fey, definitely wry, and implies underlying feelings, thoughts, ideas which are very rich indeed.

I am not sure the director, Jill Godmilow, who probably does not watch teenage movies with the avidity that I do, had any sense of what this young actor's tiny but real charm *is* on the screen. He is so understated, and she keeps posing him in Romantic ways against the car, practically with the feeling of his hair blowing in the wind. WRONG. He *isn't* Romantic on the surface; that's his strength. It is all underneath, except as glimpsed in his eyes, when WHEN he lets you see them. Any director who uses him, wastes him if she doesn't realize that.

Ah, Jonathan, I have finally allowed myself the adolescent pleasure, denied most of my life, of falling in love with the movies (and movie stars). I think I permit it now because it is so safe. Safe at my age, that is, for it wouldn't have been safe or even good or permissible when I was young. Why? Movie watching is passive, it is partly a hypnotic experience because of the music and the use of light. It might be visually stimulating but it is not intellectually stimulating. Movies also distort one's feelings about one's self because they present the human body in its most acceptable forms. Movies make us disregard or disbelieve in our own mortality, which includes our natural physical unattractiveness throughout even our youth. Movies are better than they used to be in presenting "normal looking" people, but in fact the movies which give the most satisfaction (to me) are the ones with people shown at their most attractive movie star best.

I have fought my own sentimentality, my inability to face mortality for so many years, and it has not prepared me to die after all. I guess I am letting down my guard by permitting this excessive watching of film, my only excuse being that I am excavating my past, my youth, and my possibilities. I suppose being friends with you who actually write movie scripts also gives me a sense of wanting to know more. But what is most true is that movies give me one of those parallel universes where I can live a different life than I was destined for. The life where my handsome father loved me and did not go away; where I brilliantly replaced my mother and then was courted by the nicest, richest men. Oh fairy tales, escape, oh *Purple Rose of Cairo*.

Yr Purple rose (is a rose is a rose),

Diane

SAN DIEGO

Driving my sailorfather
back to his ship
either in San Pedro with the oil wells pumping
hard and dark on Signal Hill
or in San Diego, hours of driving
through soft brown hills and the target ranges
of Camp Pendleton.

In the car, you are in
America. The silence is intimate
with each head plying/playing
the reel of fantasies. I
always want to
touch you
when we are driving
together,
my father in his uniform,
who is always
leaving me.

There was a man whose motorcycle,
perhaps an Indian from some lost, wandering tribe,
was stationed in our living room, its port,
and it was always I who left for tours of duty
returning home to his steely, wool-clad arms
until he left for the woods of Vermont

land-locked himself away
from me.

But when I sit in any car,
gliding as if I am sailing
across America, I am sure that any man
driving me
must love me,
as my father did,
though he left me so many times,
as the Motorcycle Betrayer did, though he
too could not serve as my port or starboard.

The truth is always empty.
So what?

Riding with you, whether you are Steel Man
or young Rosenkavalier, the car is woolly
with the love I knew my father
secretly had for me. Surely his favorite.
The love
which all fathers must give their
little girls,
even though they never
touch them,
except with letters coming from miles and miles
across the water.

Rose Diner
Los Angeles

Good Morning, Craig,

Thank you so much for the good feedback on my article about the expanding poetry canon. You are right that there are two arguments in the essay and one should be either eliminated or subsumed better under the big one, which is my on-going theme of what conservative times we live in and yet how hypocritically or falsely we intellectuals feel compelled to label our conservative behavior. Pretending it is a new kind of democracy or search for equality—these affirmative action anthologies—when it's not that at all. I suppose I should admire the honesty of zillionaire James Merrill in making no bones about the fact that he hates experimental writing. Still to brag about choosing a book of poems for the Yale Younger Poets award because ("what a relief! Here are poems that do not 'take risks' or 'break new ground' ") he sees the writing as old fashioned. Zillionaires must needs be conservative, I guess. They've got so much to conserve.

Well, here's a poem for you, my boy. Nobody could ever accuse you of not taking risks, though your politics which we won't discuss are quite another matter.

WAITING FOR THE NEW TOM CRUISE MOVIE: SUMMER '88

for Craig who fell over a cliff/ The Fool, in the tarot deck

Try
playing pool
with a sword. Try
remembering
the Navy pilot
who drank clear water.
Try your own
memories
of a world where all the gold
was in somebody else's
safe deposit box,
where you spoke the language
of salamanders
and listened only to *Madame Butterfly*
in English.
                    You see
what you want to see:
The Silver Surfer
out of the comics,
John Rambo, not
Arthur

unless you remember
why he gave up poetry.

And the mind is used
for many purposes:
        "what a relief," says the reviewer,
        "here are poems that do not 'take risks' or
        'break
        new ground' " Oh, Craig,
this lyric is for beautiful young men,
for you,
for Tom Cruise,
for Andrew McCarthy,
and some of the boys who sit in my
eccentric classrooms.

The woman
who has bandages on her eyes:
justice?

"O love," he says
"where are you leading me now?" But I know
where love leads us all.
To cliffs which, like the fool, we dance willingly
over. To swamps where the bad girl
from fairy tales is transformed into a Marsh King's
daughter.
To Beethoven's piano, humming and thundering
in the night or the thirty million dollar
fighter planes, where you can fly upside-down
over the enemy before drinking Pepsi,
to the place where the hoodwinked woman
stands shivering among crusader swords, and no
crusaders in sight. To eating an apple
and becoming Walt Disney's Snow White.

Love leads us, and we willingly,
lovingly follow. All our mistakes
are made for love,
or greed.
Love takes more risks
than greed.

How can we beguile ourselves?
Beauty and chaos
have the same substance,
look the same from the back;
which one is dancing ahead,
leading us,
never looking back? We turn
ourselves into coyotes,
grey and hungry,
and we follow,
running. We
follow without even thinking
it might be
a risk.

* * *

Your Lady of Safe Harbor,

DW

BAD GIRL

for Olson

She was a good
girl, a boring
girl, not the kind of Nancy
Drew she liked to read about, and
the lower half of her body always seemed to be
cut out of cardboard with dull scissors,
while her upper body was supple and sheer
like batiste, the kind that's printed with small blue
flowers and makes pretty blouses, her arms
like calla lilies.

She grew into a woman
like a bowsprit, whose upper body leaned out
towards the sea, who brought good fortune
to the men who sailed her, and like
the lady on the ship's prow
with her long tangled hair, like a
mermaid, she had
no lower body. The wood of the hull
is what that awkward cardboard lower half of her
became. With her hips and the place
where her sexual parts should have been, with her sturdy legs
and peasant feet, she sailed reliably,

175

singing, avoiding the reefs, the shoals, the
snags of utter desolation, with her voice,
the voice of a woman determined
not to wind up on the rocks.

The Lady of the Grailship, that Virgin whose female self
protects the ship and her sailors from Sirens,
the treacherous witches of the sea,
the Teeth Mother rocks, and the Medusa winds
which buffet a body to stone. Oh Olson, Oh Creeley,
Oh Dr. Williams, you follow the Indefinable.
But I am attached to the ship hip down;
I precede, but do not lead. Are you
sure that Indefinable Lady is what you should follow?
      Are you
not forgetting she might be only a wooden figure
attached to an old fashioned ship,
only a woman who can never have children,
only a wanderer who is defined
by where she goes?

                                  Ritter Cafe
                                  Vienna

Dear Jonathan,

It is clear to me now that my story, the story of
Jason and Medea, doesn't really begin until after Jason
has left Medea, married the other woman, and she has

slain her children. And I claim the version of the story in which she flees from bloody Corinth to Athens in a chariot drawn by dragons, given to her by Helios. Her magic is powerful but it did not prevent her from falling in love with Jason and leading him successfully through many dangers. When she berates Jason for betraying her love, he tells her that her love was simply a spell put on her by Aphrodite so that she would help Jason.

I have thought a lot about love and its terribleness, which for me has always been connected with sex. It is like enchantment and does not seem connected with anything that we idealize it to be. Love is the opposite of Liberty. You have no freedom whatsoever, when you are in love, and though you may have good judgment, you have no power to exercise it.

The compelling force of Medea's story is that despite her great magic (she was able to bring Jason's father back to life and to restore his youth), she was totally vulnerable to love and its betrayal. Though she escaped with her life, she lost, presumably, everything she loved. There is no way to see Medea as someone, who like Oedipus, brought on her own tragedy. She was simply a woman who loved, or was enchanted to love, and who had to live out the consequences. Perhaps that is why the stories allow her to escape, that even Euripides does not see death or exile as her tragedy, but rather the loss of everything she loves. Even though Jason is the hero of third century Apollonius of Rhodes' "The Quest of the Golden

Fleece," it is clear that he is a cad, by American standards. "Cad." Isn't that an interesting word? Comes from the French "cadet" and is related to our word "cadet."

I think the Richard Gere character in *An Officer and a Gentleman*, is a cad until his training finally forces him to understand what being a gentleman really means. In an odd way, if he were from a better family he might have been a Jason, taking what he wanted and ignoring the rules, but part of what officer's school taught him about was honor. It gave him honor. Jason had none.

Still, Jason would have thought of all of his stories as being problems to solve in the most expedient way, and by using whatever means he could. Medea's love was one expedient, just as Aeneas uses Dido to save himself from the Carthaginians and then deserts her when he needs to continue his quest. But Dido isn't a heroine any more than Medea really is. At least in literature. They are tragic women, at best. Jason and Aeneas: they're the heroes.

Some part of me will always be the betrayed woman, and that will never be seen as the heroic part of Diane. In fact, what everybody is interested in is Diane, the Sorceress, and her chariot of dragons. The woman who escaped on a Harley-Davidson: that's me. Even my kind husband, Steel Man, doesn't really care for the wounded, vulnerable Diane. At best, he humors her and tries to reassure her when she remembers the past.

MONEYLIGHT

Last night I danced alone
in my darkened living room.
Usually when I do this
I am rock 'n rolling, in a way I'd be
embarrassed to do
in public. I dance alone
because that kind of dancing doesn't
require a partner, anyway. But
last night, when I danced, I
held my hands as if they were on the
shoulder and holding the hand
of a man, a partner.
I dipped and swayed and pretended
my cheek was against his, that I was
at a dance.
That I was a different
person.
I was not happy with the thought of single dancing,
but I was almost happy, dancing with a shadow
man. This is
The King of Spain, I thought.

My husband was upstairs in his room,
working on some project or watching sports
TV. He came down once for a coke
and smiled at me. "Poor Diane," he said.

Didn't offer to dance. Went back upstairs
and left me with my teenage music
and shadow man.

What middle-age brings
is the knowledge you can never
be young again. Oddly satisfying,
once you stop being sad. You
can dance with the shadow partner
and not feel you have failed. You can
dance alone and not think it's because
there's something wrong with you. You
can invent a lover and not think
you are crazy. You can make him say all the things
your husband or lovers never said, and he'll dance
when you want to dance, and when you are tired,
you can retire to bed with your book, drink a last cup of tea,
and fall asleep next to your kind husband who whispers,
"Poor Diane," and pulls you closer like a child
to assuage you, to hold you, to love you securely, as no
      father,
as no lover, even the invisible one,
ever has.

ROBERT'S CAPS

He wears
the cap of darkness
to bed each night.
His version is a sailor's

watch cap, a black knitted glove
for the craftsman skull. Next to him
I sometimes am transformed
into the beautiful black-stockinged woman
my peasant stock did not shape,
and together we practice our marriage skills,
being invisible together
under Michigan's snowy sheets.

When we're driving,
his cap can be emblazoned like a trucker's
with words like QUALITY FARM AND FLEET
or, in the past, before he declared himself neutral,
the emblem or initials of a team, THE LIONS, perhaps
or THE STEELERS, or CARDINALS.
We call him STEEL MAN for more than his
biceps, his steely will and his reliability.

In his first self-portrait, he wore a beret;
I always thought it was too small for him,
as it didn't fold like a crepe
down over his ears, but rather
stood up, Teutonically,
like a woodchuck or a rabbit, alert
for predators, on his head. But
when he moved to Michigan, he graduated
from his preppy beret, to tweed caps
in addition to baseball hats,
finding their European wools
more adaptable to American motoring trips.

Robert believes that heat leaves
the body through the head.
Growing up in Southern California
I never wore hats, and perhaps never

conducted that childhood study in the wintery playgrounds
of where heat escapes, where it departs
from our downy selves.
I think my own life leaves through my feet,
and I stock my cupboard with extra insulation
for the bottom parts of my body.
Earthy Diane, grounded, on her feet, that's an image
of survival for me.

Robert, though, is the one who steadies
our life, in his steely arms. I touch his furnace
body-heat at night to raise my temperatures. I
pull the heat from it rising, escaping through
his head when the cap of darkness slides off
in his sleep, down, down.
My bare California feet turning icy and white
become cherub feet, as if they were encased in bunny-suit
Dr. Denton's, as Robert's Bethlehem glow
irradiates them and together we hold the heat
allowing it neither to escape from head
nor toe.

Rose Diner
Los Angeles

Dear Craig,

I just saw a fine teenage movie which I had put off
seeing because I heard such negative things about it.
It was actually reviewed as a film about teenage

182

apathy! Which is almost the exact opposite of what it is about. The movie is *River's Edge* with Dennis Hopper and a bunch of very good but unknown teenage actors and actresses. The hype of the movie is that it is about teenage apathy and how the kids don't respond to or care about the fact that one of their friends murders a girl, brags about it and brings the kids to view the body.

The truth of this movie, which is really a condemnation of the "adult" world and a very realistic portrayal of the problems of teenage life including one very sick kid—the murderer whom the others basically feel sorry for because he comes from such a desperate home that his craziness is almost forgivable—and one very screwed up kid who lives in a fantasy world reinforced by drugs and a kind of Mick Jagger-like manic energy combined with a TV version of what friendship is about, and then a bunch of normal teenagers, who have problems with normal things, like wanting to be accepted, wanting to be themselves but fearing adult authority and fearing most of all to be foolish or wrong. Thus, they seem to be very passive and uncaring. But they are more fearful than passive. The movie is about the adult failures which make them feel this way.

And this movie DOES portray what it's like to be a teenager, apart from the dramatic world of *Pretty in Pink* or *Some Kind of Wonderful* where poor kids have as much class and dignity and most of all, self-assurance as adults and rich kids do. This movie portrays something so much more real, and frankly all the hype about the movie which called it a portrayal of a decadent culture where teenage kids don't care about anything and are all totally amoral if not immoral, is so much bullshit. That IS NOT what this movie is about, at all.

What most of the critics have missed in *River's Edge* is that these teenagers are trying to be decent people (all except the murderer, who is simply crazy. He's out of it, and in fact he murders the girl because she says something unkind about his dead mother, so even he has a kind of value system, if distorted and mad.), and part of their decency is to be loyal and to respect each other's values. I found it a very touching movie, and not at all frightening, except for the violence itself, which is always frightening. But the so-called "apathy" was really respect, which perhaps was a little distorted, and fear of being disloyal to a friend. The druggy boy is hyped up on what friendship means and behaves like a criminal because he has some television idea of friendship, not because he has no values. Just the opposite. When the one boy who is the hero of the film (if that term is appropriate) finally reports the murder to the police, they hassle him for not doing it earlier, and they are so awful, you cannot imagine why the teenager even forgives them finally. What a realistic film. Very fine.

Well, I think I am finally at the stage where I can reject my adulthood almost entirely, if it has to be what is portrayed by the parents in most of these films.

There's only one teenage movie I've seen which makes me want to be an adult at all, and it is a French movie which I've forgotten the title of [*Murmur of the Heart,* directed by Louis Malle]. I saw it at one of the Classic Films showings about three or four years ago, and I wish I could remember the title, so that I could start asking for it on video. In it, a teenage boy and his mother have a wonderful sexual encounter, and it even has a happy ending, rather than the prescribed tragic one. Now, that's my kind of adulthood, even though the mother is probably only about thirty-two years old, but at least she is neither crazy, Philistine, nor just plain stupid, as most parents are. I also like *Class,* the Andrew McCarthy, Rob Lowe movie, where the boy played by McCarthy has an affair with the Rob Lowe character's mother. However, she is portrayed as rich, bored, and slightly alcoholic. A basically crazy woman, which is supposed to be the reason why she and McCarthy have this tempestuous affair. Finally, she becomes another unacceptable adult in the movie, rather than someone special and good like the teenagers. A little like Mrs. Robinson in *The Graduate.*

God, how I hate this vision of the world, that you have to lose everything as you grow older. At least you should get better in terms of human intelligence and dignity and love, but instead it seems as if you just get crazy or mean or ugly. *First Born* does a nice job of showing how tormented a mother's life can be when her husband leaves her and she tries to both give everything to her sons and then to get some satisfaction for herself. But again, in this movie, the teenager becomes the wise and gentle adult, and the mother bonkers out and practically becomes a cocaine addict. Yipes, it's enough to make you want to take cyanide before you can become a parent and to lock yourself into a room once you've passed thirty-five.

Well, Craig, you are like a son to me. Like a Knight to a Lady. You are my disciple, and I am prepared to teach you all the magic I know, though the one magic you want is the one I do not have. I am still the Medea who did not know how not to fall in love with the Jason who betrayed me. But I am also the sorceress who escaped, found another kingdom, another husband, another life. Our stories are as much our failures as our successes. Here's a spell for you, since you love hummingbirds so much.

HUMMINGBIRD LIGHT

for Jackson MacLow, Jerry & Diane Rothenberg, Carol Bergé, and Craig Cotter

In the hummingbird house
the path we take
leads everyone to a bridge. From the
roof of summer, with its wreathing vines,

186

the lips of a tropic honeysuckle,
pouting and full as a teenage girl,
offer their buckets of sap. *The Light Poems*
of Jackson MacLow are being quoted:
      "Diane in owl light,"
where does it come from, or?
      "a bulky space-suited figure"

Four of us troubadours stand on the bridge
following with our eyes these jewel engines
with their invisible wings,
but two of us are thinking of those curious poems,
The Light Poems, remembering words like "rhodocrozite."
Have I made this one up: "Carol Bergé in amber light,
     smoking a cigarette in an amber cigarette holder,
          reading *Forever*
    Amber"?
          These poems, like the utterances
of a fortune teller, make each person to whom a Light Poem
was dedicated think that Jackson knows something secret
or arcane about us. Why the owl for me? or Jack-O-Lantern
     light
for Jerry?

We are Merlin, we old poets. And Lancelot Craig,
he is too young to have a light poem written about him
by Jackson MacLow; perhaps in the hummingbird house
where he has led us, though, we could compose such a lyric.
The owl is Minerva's bird, and Merlin's. We stand on the
bridge with our old rhodocrozite eyes and amber lighted
     faces
humming these words:

FOR CRAIG WHO LEAPT OFF A CLIFF IN TO HUMMINGBIRD LIGHT

In Beatle light,
in blond white-boy light,
in fast-talking light, and lemon light,
in rose light which glows softly
or Rosenkavalier light which speeds like a train,
in the light of hummingbird wings
and the light of four gold coins,
in the light on Anna's red ears and gorgette,
in the light of the Red Cars travelling from Pasadena
to Santa Monica, in the light of August,
in pearly light or saguaro light,
in the sparkling light of eau de vie
and back to rose light or letter light
or light that sips from your knightly lips,
there is only increasing light
from the hummingbird with the long tail,
Red-tailed Comet light, Hummingbird House light,
Knight of the Rose light,
leaping off a cliff light,
sleeping in hummingbird light.

* * *

I don't know if this really constitutes irony or not,
but no marriage has ever made me a mother. I have
always been that un-wed mother. Now that I have
finally found a faithful, good husband, I am terrified
at the thought of the Jasons who defined my life. If
ageing has put me beyond them, then that is an argu-
ment for age. And I have found a son without actual
motherhood. I know it's taboo to say, but that might
be the best thing of all!

From the Sorceress,

Diane

JUNK JEWELRY

My husband buys me pearls,
the kind I like—freshwater, with their appearance
of gnarling and twisted nacre, but though
my horoscope always says I will love jewels, I
rarely deck myself with these pearls,
and I regularly over the years have lost at least one
and usually finally the second one of any pair of expensive
     gold
earrings he buys for me. He knows

I want a wedding ring,
but it is the one jewel he never will
offer. A golden heart necklace for a recent anniversary,
and the next year a diamond for it. At Christmas, a subdued
and magical pair of antique amber drops to go with
my lucky amber tear necklace on an expensive gold chain he
        gave me
the year before. He agrees that
a band of emeralds would be nice on my wedding finger,
or a thin thin line of diamonds, but we both know
that either would cost thousands and we haven't the price.
Still, I would be happy with a plain gold band
handmade by some local jeweler which might only cost
a few hundred dollars, not much more than my longest
        string
of pearls.

I ask myself many questions
about my many failures,
but one I never ask is why I fail to inspire
Steel Man to buy me a wedding ring.
I couldn't ask this question
because I think I know the answer.
It is no secret
like immortality, or who
will win the lottery. It is simple.
He buys me what no one else has ever
given me, and I had two marriages before this one
both with rings that still glitter with evil memories. Why
should he remind me of the failure of rings?

Our bond is ringless.
Nothing can break it.

Rose Diner
Los Angeles

Dear Craig,

I am not sure why I cannot let go of these betrayals.
I can only say that they are my story. And of course
the greatest betrayals were outside the actual bonds of
marriage. No, I won't say that. Those were not the
greatest betrayals. They were, rather, the most painful
losses of love. They were the experiences which finally
have allowed me to define love as something beyond
sex, though sexually charged memories still are painful
ones.

The movie script which I am going to make (Volume
III) is going to be the story of how the sorceress
escapes and reassembles her life after the betrayals.
Yes, it is the knight who delivers the lady. Either
Tom Cruise or John Cusack in the role?

The Lady in the Garden,

Diane

CHAMPAGNE

In the velvet light of Max's
Kansas City, he used to order a bottle of Veuve Cliquot each
time we met, after being separated.
The man with big shoulders who confessed that he
really liked the touch of metal; wood seemed so
much
less interesting.

Dr. Williams,
in New Jersey, was his idol.
I thought he looked for passion
in the poet's spare, tight lines,
and loved the commonness
that was
uncommon.

But poetry is about
secrets, and we love the bard
whose voice overlays some particular
which reminds us of our own taboos. The possibility of
homoeroticism
in Walt Whitman, or a hidden marriage in Emily
Dickinson's life.
I thought this man who was to become
my Motorcycle Betrayer loved
the Paterson poet because he could condense

speech
into lyric. But what he
loved
was his secret:
the many women, the sexual encounters
outside of marriage. And the loving wife,
Flossie, who bore it all and still
honored
her husband.

Champagne is the drink of weddings.
How I loved that bottle brought, as if by magic,
to our table, each time my voice had been
echoing "Spring & All,"
wanting this man to marry me,
accepting instead the celebratory drink
of marriages, the toasts, the making love.

But he left me,
he left me.
I was no Flossie,
I could not share.

The search for Persephone —
she draws any man who loves her beauty
down, down, underground.
Like Eve, she eats a blood-red fruit.
Like Eve, she is naked and lovely.

But there are women,
and I am one of them,
who sit only
in our gardens and wait
for the wedding glass of champagne
to be offered.

It appears sometimes, floating in
the distance, as the Grail did
to Sir Percival.

I thank all the men in my life
who have offered me a crystal cup of champagne
with the understanding that I am neither Persephone nor
      Eve;
that I cannot leave the Garden,
that to drink is final,
a cup of blood, a cup of light—it
cannot alter
the truth.

                                    Ritter Cafe
                                    Vienna

Dear Jonathan,

When next we meet, it will be at the Mailbag Cafe
in Las Vegas, because what we are going to do is
work out a movie together. I need the hand of the
master magician. That's you. Until then, let me leave
you with my thanks for *Child Across the Sky* and help-
ing me to understand a little about evil.

Your still very vulnerable sorceress,

Diane (Moon)

194

Cafe Eau de Vie
Michigan

Dear Craig, Dear Jonathan, Dear Reader,

This is the end of Volume I. The threads of the story
are all here. Liberty, Love, Luck, they are all Ladies.
I am another,

Yrs,

Diane (Moon)

FAILURES OF THE WORLD

for Judith Minty

This body is first
among its failures.
The perfect fur of the kitten
turning to lumpy rags, the clean matted
roughness of a rug, the holes

195

which trip walkers, and finally require
the rug be discarded.

I dreamed last night
but I refuse to say
what I dreamed. I can go
no farther than to wake up
hating my body. The cat's claws
unsheathed, but even blood
seems fresh, a refreshing form
of death.

Compared to what I
imagined.
             I didn't dream this:
but I know the skeletons of poets
sometimes wear the dress or garb
of a beautiful woman.
Those long sapphire skirts
make you think that a white foot
of pure skin and flower fresh
runs quickly under them. But the
velvet shoes rather than holding
a pink-tipped line of plum-soft toes,
hold nothing. Worse than nothing,
an old body.

I once saw a famous but
unkempt man barefooted.
His toenails were like spikes
jetting out from surprisingly soft
white feet. I thought death
was walking towards me.
I wondered about innocence,
but I, last night,

in my dream saw something
which makes me know that myths/
religions have not made us fear sex
enough, have not shown us
that beauty is not possible
without deceit.

The dawn, the sunrise, this cup
of coffee I drink with my son,
my father, my brother, my lover or husband
or friend—deceit.
And now, for once, I beg
that disappearing figure
I no longer want ever to see,
to trick me, to beguile me,
to let me think
once again
the new is pure,
there is a soft white foot
which made Sappho's print,
that it *is*
Love
which leads me
and not Death.

My sister
in her wooden cabin
feeds the birds apples,
loves her old black dog
and uses the animals
for her disguise.
She is the photo which deflects death,
her portrait clearly showing an alternative
to the beauty of youth in the hawk talon
    around her neck.

I have no alternative yet,
so the dream is
unacceptable. Men see me
as a snake, not an animal with soft paws. Hot
deserts are where I thrive. What if I were the one
to eat the apple, rather than offer it?

No, there is nothing
if I believe my dream. So,
I will never tell it. The truth,
if it is the truth, is one of those failures
of the world.

* * *

Printed November 1990 in Santa Barbara & Ann
Arbor for the Black Sparrow Press by Graham
Mackintosh & Edwards Brothers Inc. Text set in
Bembo by Words Worth. Design by Barbara Martin.
This edition is published in paper wrappers;
there are 400 hardcover trade copies;
150 copies have been numbered & signed
by the poet; & 50 numbered copies with an
original holograph poem have been handbound
in boards by Earle Gray & are signed by the poet.

Photo: Robert Turney

DIANE WAKOSKI was born in Whittier, California in 1937 and educated at U.C., Berkeley. She has published eighteen full-length collections of poems and many other slim volumes. Her two most recent collections from Black Sparrow are *Emerald Ice: Selected Poems 1962–1987* (1988) which won the Poetry Society of America's William Carlos Williams Award in 1988, and *Medea the Sorceress* (1990). She is currently Writer in Residence at Michigan State University.